IN
MYSTERY

LIVING
IN
MYSTERY

Ruth Burrows

SHEED & WARD
LONDON

ISBN 0–7220–5095–X

Published in Great Britain by
Sheed & Ward Limited
14 Coopers Row
London EC3N 2BH

Designed and typeset by Bill Ireson

Printed and bound in Great Britain by Biddles Limited,
Guildford and Kings Lynn

This book is dedicated to
Peter
Bishop of the Church of God
in
East Anglia

Foreword

To love God, to let Jesus possess us and surrender us to the Father in the Holy Spirit: this is not easy, but it is exceedingly simple. That is the trouble, because such stark simplicity gives the ego no hiding place. If we truly believed that the Father is as Jesus has described, Total Love, then to be possessed by this love should not alarm us, but all too often it does: our belief is unconsciously half-hearted.

A long life of spiritual reading has convinced me (though perhaps I have only my own obtuseness to blame) that there are very few writers who understand the Mystery of God and the absoluteness with which Jesus has shared with us all he is. Julian of Norwich understands, she who 'chose Jesus to be her heaven' and so does St Teresa of Avila and St Therese of Lisieux. To these names we can add another, Ruth Burrows. Here we have the unmistakable note of living faith. Here is one who has been overpowered by Jesus and has found the clear and earnest words that communicate her knowledge. It is a living knowledge, not so much felt as lived. Burrows has always been certain that what we feel may be only subjective, our flawed reaction to Mystery. It is what we know, not of ourselves but in Jesus that is unflawed and everlasting.

This book is not easy reading, elegant though it is in style. If we seek consolation, to feel safe within the small pool of our achievements, our virtue, then Burrows can be disconcerting. She wants us to be drawn out of safe

havens into the great ocean of Truth, where we are transformed. She does what we are told to do in Hebrews: she
never takes her eyes off Jesus, our Pioneer. Looking at
him, we have no time to look too anxiously at self. We
are changed into his glory, not by one concentrated act
after another, but almost as a by-product, as we 'press forward'. Burrows dares her all upon the confidence that
God is Father, in a sense that only the Son fully knew or
could know, and this conviction irradiates everything she
writes. It irradiates us, too, as we read: may we all share
with her this blessed transformation into that freedom
which is the free gift of the Spirit.

Sister Wendy Beckett

LIVING
IN
MYSTERY

Such inexhaustible comfort

Such certain hope

Preface

It is more than twenty years since I wrote *Before the Living God*. A lot of water has flowed under the bridge in the intervening years. The stones and mortar of the bridge have not changed, its form is the same and likewise the landscape in which it is set. But the water? What can be said of the water? The debris it carries: life's events, thoughts, ideas, emotions, actions and reactions – these can be looked at and described, but the water itself is God's secret, God's own life flowing within. Always – and this is an aspect of ourselves as mystery – what is of most significance, what is most truly ourselves, escapes our detection, at a level not normally available to our conscious mind. We are indeed creatures of mystery, drawing 'from out the silent deep' and flowing back into it as to our home.

The longer I live the more I experience that God is Absolute Mystery, and as I grow in perception of this, I perceive also the sheer simplicity and unity of life. There is thus an increasing sense of 'unknowing' even though, as far as I can see, I do grow in wisdom and understanding.

However, this sense of 'unknowing' annulled any desire to write, for what was there to say? Recently, it dawned on me that this very insight is important and needs to be communicated, and this has been confirmed by conversations with some unbelievers (in that they could not ascribe to any creed). Furthermore, it has always been a

3

grief to me to read in the press and in literature in general, popular views of what Christians are supposed to believe and Catholic Christians in particular.

What a caricature! We Christians cannot deny all responsibility for this. Only too easily do we fail to see the wood for the trees and hardly give the impression that God is the overwhelming reality of our lives and of the religion we profess. Our somewhat facile 'God-talk' can, to the sincere and fundamentally religious spirit, seem irreverent if not blasphemous. 'How can one talk of God like that?', they exclaim, and rightly so.

All this woke in me an urge to highlight if I could, the essential of our faith, to stress over and over again the one thing we know with absolute certainty, given to us in Jesus our Lord, that Word, that Truth, of such completion that it leaves no more to be said: Jesus Christ, the presence of God's love. It takes all the courage I have to pursue my aim. A sense of absurdity comes over me and a text beats in my brain:

> Who is this that darkeneth counsel by words without knowledge?[1]

Am I playing with words irreverently, trying to give verbal expression to that before which silent adoration alone is appropriate?

> O Lord, thou hast searched me, and known me![2]

I trust in the love that has come to us in humble human form and addressed us in human words, and, further, I take courage from the words of Pope John Paul II which have come timely to my notice:

> The women and men of today are asking us to show
> them Christ, who knows the Father and has revealed him

4

. . . we are called to show in word and deed today the immense riches that our churches preserve in the coffers of their tradition.[3]

The riches in our coffers, the purest, the unflawed, simple treasures are often overlaid, embellished in such a way that they are lost to view.

Everything I write in this book arises from my own conviction and I say nothing that I do not believe to be true. I am not academically minded but have read much, though only for the sake of spiritual profit. I acknowledge an immense debt to theologians and biblical scholars in particular. These latter have enabled me to expose myself more immediately to the holy Mystery of Jesus Christ. Karl Rahner's essay, 'The Concept of Mystery in Catholic Theology',[4] continues to inspire me. There I found, long years ago, conceptual expression for what I hold to be my deepest convictions. More recently, Catherine Mowry LaCugna in her profound study of Trinitarian theology, *God for Us*,[5] has led me to the luminous truth: 'Communion is the nature of ultimate reality',[6] which is, of course, a commentary on the biblical summary of revelation: 'God is love.'[7]

Finally, my very special thanks go to Mark Allen, my friend, who read and reread my rough draft with infinite care and fulfilled the role of a skilful tutor as I set about the revision. I had complete confidence not only in his natural ability but in his spiritual understanding, for he is one who watches daily at wisdom's door.

1

Holy Mystery. That has become my chosen way of speaking of ultimate reality. To say 'God' is already to introduce revelation. 'God' is a relational term and that it can be used of the holy Mystery, that the holy Mystery offers to be our God, we know only through revelation. The world, of itself, does not reveal God. Even so, our God remains total Mystery, inaccessible to the created intellect, indefinable. To speak of absolute Being is to reduce that of which we speak to the level of something of which we have experience – being. 'Mystery', I suggest, leaves our subject outside all categories, beyond the range of words and concepts, stretching to infinitude. At least, it seems to me, the best we can do is to refuse definition or description.

> Man is the being of the holy Mystery. Man is he who is confronted with the holy Mystery even when dealing with what is within hand's reach, comprehensible, amenable to the conceptual framework. So the holy Mystery is not something upon which we may 'also' (among other things) stumble if we are lucky and take an interest in something else besides the definable objects within the horizon of consciousness. As human beings we always live by the holy Mystery even when not conscious of it.[1]

It is the innate drive of the mystery that is ourselves – finite indeed, with a finitude that assaults and wounds us at every

7

turn – to reach out everlastingly, to know more and more so as to realise our own infinitude.

> The basis of human thought is something that has not
> been contrived by human beings. Perhaps this is in itself
> an indication that truth is to be found not so much in
> our responsive language as in that which causes us to ask
> questions, and our conscious ignorance . . . Growth in
> experience comes, when our plans and reflections, our
> anticipation of knowledge, come up against the refractory
> nature of reality which thus reveals itself indirectly. This
> resistance directs all our reflection. It reveals a reality
> which is independent of all human plans, which does not
> come from humans but from 'elsewhere' . . .
> Relationship to the unconscious (i.e. the unknown) and
> the inexpressible, is an essential part of critical human
> reason.[2]

Wherever we turn our eyes, wherever our minds stray, we are confronted with mystery. Human beings have always been implicitly aware of the mysterious nature of reality and, with their religious beliefs and rites, have tried to come to terms with it, gain some control over the mystery, ensure its good will and ward off its awful power. The Old Testament is the story of a people's effort to deal with mystery. We find in its pages almost every ploy that human beings use to impose order on chaos, give meaning to what is meaningless and to control by knowledge. But over and over again these efforts are defeated by reality which is not what they would like it to be and refuses to fit into their patterns of thought. Even so, this people had courage to believe in what we call revelation: that the incalculable, the unutterable Mystery had in some way 'spoken' to them, had not left them defenceless and in total ignorance.

Holy Mystery had revealed itself to be their own God

who made demands indeed, but who cared. By a series of mighty deeds, they had been rescued from ignominious slavery, forged into a people and given a land of their own. The sense of election gave them identity as a people, the 'people God has chosen as his own'. What was privilege and responsibility became self-glorification, an indisputable claim over God, a reduction of holy Mystery to a god, a human projection of sinful hearts. We can perceive through the bible the human propensity to 'tame', make manageable the holy Mystery, whereby God is no longer independent reality but a 'derivation from the existence of Jerusalem',[3] and always there comes the reaction, the corrective vision, the prophet's pen scouring through illusion, asserting once again the uncontrollable, utterly free, holy Mystery.

There is one writer in particular who, I think, bears strong kinship to our own sceptical culture − Quoheleth, or Ecclesiastes, as he is sometimes called. His intriguing testament seems to be a broadside aimed at conventional wisdom insofar as this had rounded itself off, assuming it had the answers and the key to the management of life. It is our human propensity, always at war with our restless yearning, to grow weary of mystery, and so we start defining boundaries and establishing certainties. So cuts the sword of Quoheleth:

> . . . all is vanity and a striving after wind . . . I said to myself, 'I have acquired great wisdom, surpassing all who were over Jerusalem before me; and my mind has had great experience of wisdom and knowledge.' . . . 'I perceived that this also is but a striving after wind.'[4]

Quoheleth runs through a gamut of human experience: the 'test of pleasure', of possessions, of greatness and of wisdom and all was 'striving after wind': its procession of seasons, the way human beings are, the injustices of fate, the enigma of suffering and of death for him, without rhyme or reason.

> When I applied my mind to know wisdom, and to see the business that is done on earth . . . then I saw all the work of God, that man cannot find out the work that is done under the sun. However much man may toil in seeking, he will not find it out; even though a wise man claims to know, he cannot find it out.[5]

No one can stand inside the mind of another person and view the world as that person views it. It is impossible to identify with another's experience and we have no certitude that our most sensitive perceptions regarding another are accurate. Nevertheless, I find myself baffled by what seems a purely pragmatic approach to life. Many people seem to skim over life's surface, people who command respect. Good as they are, they appear not to reflect at all upon the ultimate meaning. It seems that day-to-day living, with its tasks, events, relationships, pleasures, disappointments, defines the circumference of their experience and suffices. The ultimate questions do not impinge. Are they this by temperament or choice, a choice perhaps made long ago, half-consciously, because too close a scrutiny of life would prove unbearable? Do they, in fact, by force of habit, repel the first urge to stand still and reflect? I do not know. Such an attitude need not be irreligious. To admit defeat before impenetrable mystery could be a sort of humility. Quoheleth concludes that the only wise thing to do is simply to live in this opaque, ambiguous world, doing what has to be done, eating, drinking, enjoying whatever pleasure life has to offer, for life is short. It is folly to waste time and energy on unanswerable questions. Maybe there are more Quoheleths abroad in our times than we know of, but the biblical sage really exposed himself to impenetrable mystery and suffered the consequence. His approach, for all its seeming negativity and cynicism, is profoundly religious.

We, of course, do not fall on our knees in worshipful dread of lightning or the crash of thunder, nor are we likely to give credence to claims that the Deity reveals itself in dreams and visions. But can it be said that our scientific knowledge has brought us at least to the frontiers from which there is no further on, that the universe is emptied of mystery, its contents spread before us, categorised, labelled and that everything is explicable? Still less can we claim to have gained total control since reality is now as we perceive it to be and the reins are firmly in our omnipotent grasp?

There is a strain of Quoheleth in myself and I have no difficulty empathising with those who cannot explicitly affirm the existence of God. I too stall before the expression 'existence of God'. At the same time, I wholly identify with Karl Rahner:

> The mystery is the one thing that is self-explanatory, the one thing that is its own sufficient reason . . . it has always been familiar to us and we have always loved it.[6]

I recall with emotion a little incident recorded in the original manuscript of my book *Before the Living God*, but which was omitted from the published edition. Searching for self-understanding at the time, I had sent a snapshot of myself as a child of seven or eight to Elsa, my friend and counsellor. Elsa responded:

> This is a child made for tears, a child naked to reality, suffering, bewildered, quivering, a pathetic smile to propitiate the mystery round her. A small, closed world of fear and pain.[7]

Clearly, this child did not love mystery!

Mystery was not comforting. In my book, I tried to show how that child, as she grew into adolescence and adulthood, fought to meet pain and fear, to accept reality and live with mystery (which, in her case, consisted largely in the unrelieved silence and unresponsive hiddenness of God) whilst all the while that God was capturing her heart in such a way that she was obsessed with the God that was not there for her! And with profound gratitude I see the circle complete: the child as I was, shrouded painfully in mist that for her had no luminosity, become the old woman that I now am, for whom, or so I believe,

> the incomprehensibility of God is the definitive blessing, the alpha and omega of reality, behind which there is nothing and before which there can be nothing.[8]

A woman who knows

> the grace of loving the darkness without reserves . . . with the divinely given courage to enter the bliss which is authentic and unique and to enjoy it as the nourishment of the strong.[9]

It seems to me that what I understand to be my 'I' has been thrown up helpless on the banks of the tidal river flowing deep within. Is the estuary river or sea? Thought can raise a sceptical eyebrow, emotion remain coldly unresponsive, and all the 'I' can do is trust. 'Acts' of trust seem emasculated, no more than the chirping of a tired bird. All energy, all attention are absorbed into the waters flowing there without the 'I', with a momentum all their own and this, I know, is my real life, a life that is not 'mine'.

Each of us has a unique vocation most likely conditioned by our natural temperament – or shall we say that our natural temperament mysteriously forms part of our vocation? My vocation is no more unique than that of anyone else and for all I know many people may feel as I do. However, it does seem to me that I have been called to experience and accept human reality in a sharp way. It is not an easy vocation but possibly it enables me to discern rather clearly the naked structure of the human vocation which is, of course, the Christian vocation. My life in Carmel has aided and abetted this clarification for, as I understand it, Carmel exists for the purpose of enabling persons to live at great depth, naked before the living God. I treasure the insight but I have come to realise that it carries the disadvantage perhaps of my not being sufficiently there where people actually are and therefore misunderstanding and being misunderstood. Years of attention to others, trying with all my heart to empathise with them have, I hope, developed a greater awareness. Be that as it may, I earnestly desire that what I offer resonates with faith in others, with respect and compassion.

For none of us is experience of Mystery unreservedly comforting. Far from it. Each of us must anxiously question as I did: Is this inescapable, self-evident (once we think about it) mystery, 'holy Mystery'? Will it catch me as I fall? Can it be relied upon to care for me? I found my answer where it is there for all of us, in 'the surpassing knowledge of Jesus Christ', and in that and that alone can we have the courage to live consistently in mystery, refusing to give way to fear, because in Jesus we have the assurance that mystery is indeed holy Mystery, all-encompassing, all-sufficing beauty and love. The older I become, the more I grasp that the what, the who, whom we call God is totally other and that, if we are to be true to ourselves and loyal to the holy Mystery, we must accept to live without certainties and cease craving for them. We have one, all-sufficing certainty: God is love.

13

God in God's essence is totally unknowable. Yes. But I know that this same Mystery can be 'known' and that the answer to all our yearning, our questioning, the fulfilment of our transcendence, is utterly close, intimate, available, not to thought or to emotion but to love. The 'unattainable' is not a closed door but a welcome, a heart wide open to receive us. Through Jesus I know that the holy Mystery is not something but someone, not merely fullness of being but also and primarily fullness of love, a holy communion opening itself outwards to embrace all persons, gathering all home to itself.

I believe it is the Christian vocation, through its faith in Jesus, not merely to cut deeply through life's waters but to abandon ship, so to speak, and surrender fully to Mystery. It is a vocation and vocation calls for a life-long commitment in a surrender to the divine action we call grace. It is possible simply because we are loved.

With all the passion of my heart I declare Jesus, the crucified and risen one, to be the alpha and omega of all things, the first-born of creation, the holy Mystery's self-communication, the definitive Word of how and what that Mystery is to us; in J. A. T. Robinson's felicitous expression, he is the 'human face of God'[10] turned towards us in ineffable friendliness. Jesus is nothing less than God-given for us. He is the true light enlightening every human person whether that person knows it or not. With trembling gratitude I humbly claim to be among those who have seen with their own eyes, touched, handled the Word that is life – the eternal life that was with the Father and is now with us.[11]

As Christians we hold only one certainty: God's unconditional love. But we live in space and time, in history, responding to reality in its manifold forms. If the pure, white light is to be loved by us and if we are to choose it of our own free will as our true home, it must pass through a prism and be broken up into different colours, not to deceive or decoy us but to increase our yearning for the source of its beauty. In Catholic piety we speak of the mysteries of Jesus' life on which we are invited to meditate. The liturgical season revolves around them: Jesus' birth, his presentation in the Temple, his temptations in the desert, his passion, death and resurrection. Contemplation of each of these separate mysteries opens us more profoundly to the one holy Mystery of which these are reflections. If we look into dogmas, try to understand what the Church means by them, we shall perceive that these too are ways in which the love of God for us is revealed.

For example, take the Marian dogmas of the Immaculate Conception and Assumption. These, to some people, can seem extraneous to the holy Mystery, pious wishful thinking which has no right to be deemed certainty. What, in fact, we find in both dogmas is a revelation of the holy Mystery's loving purpose for humankind. In this one woman we see the mystery of what it means to say that we are chosen in Christ

> before the foundation of the world, that we should be holy and blameless before him.[12]

And for those whom he foreknew he also predestined to be conformed to the image of his Son:

> And those whom he predestined he also called; and those whom he called he also justified; and those whom he justified he also glorified.[13]

Each of us may take these words to ourselves. Each of us, if we choose to receive the grace offered, can cry with Mary that the Lord has clothed us head to foot in his salvation, thrown around us the cloak of his love, and made us holy.[14]

Again, a careful examination of the dogma of purgatory would yield further insight into the Mystery of love that is both purifying and transforming.

Everything that the Church holds and teaches as truth is an elaboration of the one truth, a human attempt, under the guidance of the Holy Spirit, to draw out its implications so that it becomes the supreme reality of our lives. Inevitably, human weakness can obscure the truth. What is perfectly intelligible in one culture may be unintelligible in another; but, sooner or later, again under the Spirit's guidance, this will be corrected as we have many times seen. Christianity when it is really true to itself, brings us to the point of obedient surrender – call it faith, call it love, when, rejecting every other security, we cast ourselves into the divine abyss, or stand exposed to unfiltered light. It is right for non-Christians to spurn, what seems to them, fantastic information regarding the Deity and

> atheism is an eloquent spokesman for divine transcendence . . . [it] is a purification of man-made ideas of God.[15]

The intelligent and shrewd easily detect in religious people the immature, if wholly understandable, longing for certainties, whether in what to believe or in what to do or not do. There are many who consciously scorn this make-believe and prefer to live without hope rather than bolster themselves with illusion.

Faith is not immune to the assaults of doubt but rather refined by them. To stand on the God Jesus reveals, means that we do not bury our head in the sand but submit to the hammer blows of modern life's complexities, its technology and ever-expanding knowledge, as well as to the appalling horrors that technology has made immediate to us. Faith refuses to be dismayed by increasing secularisation. A faith that is shattered by anything that can transpire in this world, is not faith in the holy Mystery but only in our poor notions and images. Secularisation, far from being the foe of Christianity and the enemy of truth, is their ally, allowing us to point to nothing as proof of God's presence and action. A God that can be proved or disproved, by the very nature of things, cannot be God, the transcendent Mystery. It is God's positive will that men and women create the world and assume responsibility for it, even though it never escapes God's everlasting care.

The advance of science cannot undermine faith if faith is real. Occasions when we do find ourselves shaken are opportunities to reflect on our understanding of God. We are sure to find that we are putting God alongside other things: supreme, beyond imagination, but still, basically, an object that, however transcendentally, bears relation to other objects. This is, of course, no God. God is not an object. The transcendent can never be investigated by science either for affirmation or denial. All we can ever lose is our own projections of God and this loss, painful though it may be at the time, is a blessing. We can no more eliminate the holy Mystery than we can eliminate the horizon. No matter how far we reach, the horizon is there ahead, unconquerable and ever beckoning. We can never find ourselves on the other side and thereby prove its grand illusion. The holy Mystery is the unconquerable horizon of our thought, of our aspiration and longing for happiness. Were the inconceivable to happen and we leaped over to the other side, thought itself would be annihilated and so would all desire and, like the spellbound of fairy tale, we would be turned to stone.

We may not like aggressive secularisation, we may dislike intensely some of its effects feeling that, in spite of its immense blessings, it is creating a hard-edged, unlovely world. Even so, as Christians we may not condemn and reject it in itself. Of course, sin is at work here, sin as unbridled greed, selfishness and lack of responsibility, but no more so probably than it has ever been present in human affairs. We may rightly fear the fact that now this greed and selfishness handle formidable power to exploit and destroy on a massive scale. As Christians, called to live in reality (for only here are we exposed to the holy Mystery), we may not indulge in nostalgia in the sense that we refuse to live wholeheartedly in the world as it is now. It is in the now, whether we like this now or not, that we must surrender in obedience to God, and so we work with divine love to transform this present world into that mystery called in scripture 'the kingdom of God'.

The holy Mystery is love. Can we assume that we know what we mean by this assertion? Love is one of those human words so full of meaning that it defies definition. Love is experience and experience as varied as there are persons to experience. What do we mean when we speak of God's love for us? It certainly is not obvious; not obvious in the way that we perceive human love. Perhaps we can feel our way towards an answer thus: the infinite Mystery, the all 'behind which there is nothing and before which there is nothing' offers its very self to us as our completion and total happiness. God's love, then, means God's unreserved self-donation to us, and our receiving this, becoming filled with the fullness of God, is the only possible human fulfilment. What follows is the guarantee that, if we accept, ultimately, 'not a hair of your head will perish' our personal existence is affirmed, loved into total happiness. God's love can be utterly relied on to bring us this final bliss; nothing whatever can prevent it except our own choice, and everything we need will be at hand. Whatever it seems like we are not tossed around by fate. Each of us is a history of salvation being written by God. As our final end is beyond our grasp so are the mysterious workings of divine love to achieve this end. We are called to trust in the love that is totally devoted to us and can be relied on absolutely; that this holy Mystery, this indestructible horizon is pure, nurturing love I know only through Jesus. Without him, I, most certainly, could not know it.

The face of reality is unreliable, at one time smiling, at another stonily indifferent and, not infrequently, savagely threatening. Suffering remains an impenetrable mystery and as Christians we make no claim to explain it. It is there for all of us, a dark veil smothering the divine Face of beauty, goodness and love. Why? Why? Why? 'You are indeed a God who lies hidden', and there is no thicker shroud than that of suffering.

2

Suffering is an aspect of death; an assault upon human well-being. We are made for happiness we feel, and who can prove us wrong? Why our endless searching for contentment unless it is there for us, somewhere? It is not only that we never wholly find it even in our greatest joy, but that, round every corner suffering lurks in one form or another. We feel outraged by this constant thwarting of our deepest longings. And, finally, there comes that dreadful destruction we call death. Unless God can deal with this, give a satisfactory answer, redeem us from our incompleteness, our finitude, and our total loss in death, God is not God, not 'our God'. Any concept we have of an Absolute turned towards us in love, has to be questioned on death in all its manifestations. If we are to have meaning, if we are not the flotsam of some fantastic fluke that happened to happen – demanding an infinitely greater leap of faith than belief in our meaningful origin in love – then our God must guarantee for us an absolute future. In Jesus and Jesus only we have the certainty that God does so.

Preserved within the pages of the Old Testament is the drama of a people's struggle with the mystery of suffering and in particular the suffering of the righteous. We can read how it was that defeat, conflict with other nations, disaster, affliction smelted down and forged anew and ever anew, their understanding of God. The catastrophe of all catastrophes, that which seemed to hold within itself every affliction, was the destruction of Jerusalem and the razing of the Temple by the army of Nebuchadnezzar, king of Babylon. This was a blow at their very identity as a nation and as the people of God; one could say that their God died in the tomb of the Temple ruins. This calamity above all others was the catalyst for a renewed search, with chastened, purified gaze, for the true face of God. The books of the bible as we have them are the work of people, or the work of their heirs, who themselves endured the ordeal and the deportations to Babylon that followed it. This break, this 'death' lies at the heart of the bible, as its dynamism. The ancient myths and traditions, ancestral legends, royal chronicles, the writings and oral traditions of the great prophets, all must now be seen from this vantage point, through the lens of this death and new possibility. Similarly with the New Testament: we have the evangelists, decades after the events concerning Jesus, taking hold of the traditions, oral or written, and interpreting them in the light of the Resurrection. Although the remnant of the exiles was resettled in their own land and the Temple was rebuilt, nevertheless, Judah was never again an independent kingdom; the glories of the Davidic and Solomonic empire had been 'swept away like a dream'. The truly spiritual element saw in this a holy providence. This 'poor and humble people' was free now to 'seek the Lord' and find God as God really is. But the bible is nothing if it is not a record of how human beings actually are and how difficult it is for them to accept the light, to receive God on God's terms. We find our own intransigence mirrored there.

Men and women of faith refused an atheistic interpretation of what was, on the face of it, a mere historical fact: another small nation despoiled and taken over by aggressive Babylon. There was a simple, if terrible, explanation that faith discerned: the apostasy of Israel. The pre-exilic prophets fulminate against national transgression. The people's flouting of the law and covenant, their trading on the privilege of being the Lord's own people, the Lord who was majestically enthroned in their Temple, and completely ignoring the responsibilities of their election. They could not say they had not been warned! The prophets are emphatic, speaking on behalf of God. Divine patience is at an end. God has had enough, God's wrath descends in the iron hand of Babylon, the flood comes to drown the world they know, corrupt as it is. The writer of Genesis knows the answer to the 'Why?':

> The Lord saw that the wickedness of man was great in the earth, and that every imagination of the thought of his heart was only evil continually. And the Lord was sorry that he had made man on the earth, and it grieved him to his heart. So the Lord said: 'I will blot out man whom I have created from the face of the earth . . . for I am sorry that I have made him.'[1]

Rough justice, but fair enough! It is something we can understand and therefore does not oblige us to a confrontation with mystery. Purifying, chastening, indeed, but still, it is the action of a God we can deal with. We have learned our lesson, the people might think, and now we know the consequences of transgression. If we keep the law and act righteously we can be sure that everything will go well with us.

> I have been young, and now I am old; yet I have not seen the righteous forsaken or his children begging bread. Wait for the Lord, and keep to his way, and he will exalt you to possess the land.[2]

No matter how justified the principle of just retribution applied to the people as a whole, in face of the destruction of the nation, nevertheless it is too easy, too generalised an answer to satisfy a heart that searches for the truth. Within the bible itself protesting voices are raised. Reality is not simple, reality denies facile solutions. What of the innocent? Were all the men and women of Sodom corrupt? Does the machinery of war discriminate between the just and the unjust? Besides, is not enough enough? We have suffered severely and long. Will God never forgive? Does the Lord's wrath remain unappeased?

> All this has come upon us, though we have not forgotten thee, or been false to thy covenant. Our heart has not turned back, nor have our steps departed from thy way.[3]

The naïve and comforting – only if you are not the sufferer – view that affliction in itself is a proof of guilt and good fortune of virtue, was challenged. The author of the book of Job is perhaps the chief protagonist. He has his Job strive with this mysterious God who does not keep the rules; Job laments, he rages and bitterly, stubbornly rejects the hollow assumption that the righteous are never forsaken. He is righteous, and he is forsaken!

Life is just, contends traditional piety, and this, of course, means God, the controller of events, is just. The good have it good, the bad have it bad. Job himself had lived complacently with this bland assumption

> . . . in the months of old, as in the days when God watched over me; when his lamp shone upon my head and by his light I walked through darkness; as I was in my autumn days, when the friendship of God was upon my tent; when the Almighty was yet with me.[4]

And, of course, this was expected for had Job not lived blamelessly, a model of compassion? Why then this incomprehensible weight of affliction? It is to his credit that he refuses to take the escape route offered him and admit he is guilty. Everyone is guilty, everyone has secret sins. Surely Job can agree to that and see his suffering as God's chastening hand? So, in substance, speak his friends, the proponents of conventional platitudes.

'No!' says Job. 'No! I will defend my ways to his face!'

Nothing Job has done deserves such punishment. Job prefers to stay with the Mystery; he is allowing reality to purify his concepts of God. His landmarks may be destroyed but he will not erect new ones, he would rather face the featureless expanse of ocean and wait for the answer.

In both the Old and New Testaments we see how hard it is for human beings to live with mystery, to surrender a notion of God whose action they can understand. It seems that they find it easier to assume guilt and see suffering as retribution rather than stay exposed to the sheer Mystery of the incomprehensible, uncontrollable, unpredictable God. Jesus' own disciples, who lived in his company, proved intractable on this score even to the end.

We still hear from Christians today: 'What have I done to deserve this? I have tried to live a good life, why has God done this to me?'

There is perhaps no greater demonstration of this evasion of mystery than the ending of the book of Job as we have it. Some devout scribe found the 'unsatisfactory' answer, which was no answer in the sense of explanation, too much. He stepped in to supply the happy ending. Job is rewarded twice over, with rich presents of gold, vast herds of cattle, sons and daughters in abundance:

> . . . and in all the land there were no women so fair as Job's daughters.[5]

We may take satisfaction in that Job learned something new from his trials for behold, the unthinkable!

And their father gave them [his daughters] inheritance among their brothers.[6]

One discerns in the book of Job and in the psalms of lament that the deepest affliction was the sense that suffering itself signified the loss of divine companionship.

Lo, he passes by me, and I see him not; he moves on, but I do not perceive him.[7]

It is this loss that makes Job's other sufferings quite unbearable. He begins to realise this, that if only he had the assurance that he was not forgotten by God – that, in the end, God would show he wanted him – he could bear his present afflictions with patience.

Thou wouldest call, and I would answer thee; thou wouldest long for the work of thy hands.[8]

We can see the paradox of faith being put to the test. On the one hand, the sufferers believe they have been abandoned by God; but, on the other hand, it is to this very God they turn when all human help has failed. Their lonely hearts reach out in the darkness for God's secret presence. The heart has a deeper wisdom than the head. This wisdom, with its tender light, can prove stronger than the muffling fogs of an all-too-human religious sophistry. The very struggle, agonising though it is, brings them to a deeper assurance, resting not on their own experience, not on their innocence but on the certainty of the Lord's faithfulness and love.

But as for me, my feet had almost stumbled, my steps had well nigh slipped. For I was envious of the arrogant, when I saw the prosperity of the wicked.[9]

And:

> Nevertheless I am continually with thee; thou dost hold
> my right hand. Thou dost guide me with thy counsel,
> and afterward thou wilt receive me to glory. Whom have
> I in heaven but thee? And there is nothing upon earth
> that I desire besides thee. My flesh and my heart may fail,
> but God is the strength of my heart and my portion for
> ever.[10]

The book of Isaiah throws its own mysterious light on
the innocent sufferer. We are given an unforgettable,
haunting picture of a man of sorrows, bowed down with
grief, so bruised, so broken, so humiliated as to seem
scarcely human. He is innocent. Unequivocal is the equa-
tion between punishment and guilt. This is punishment
for iniquity and it is the Lord's own doing: the man is
'smitten by God', but – and here lies the hitherto
unknown thing:

> For that which has not been told them they shall see; and
> that which they have not heard they shall understand.[11]

And:

> He was wounded for our transgressions, he was bruised
> for our iniquities . . . and the Lord has laid on him the
> iniquity of us all.[12]

We cannot explain how suffering is redemptive, and
more especially vicarious suffering. It was this venerable,
mysterious figure of the man of sorrows that enabled the
first Christians to sustain in faith the remembrance of the
terrible humiliation, suffering and defeat of their Lord,
that the experience of the risen One itself could not

soften. That the Messiah should undergo so appalling a fate was, for Jews, a massive stumbling block.

In Jesus all human concepts of God were revealed as hollow: God's dealing with his beloved, his perfect one in whom was refuted forever the notion that suffering is God's punishment for sin.

> He committed no sin; no guile was found on his lips.[13]

There was no demonstrable saving intervention in the passion of Jesus; no angel to stay the executioner's hand, no miraculous darkness to allow escape, no pretended dying but only total loss, total defeat. Answer there was, but not of this world and one that offered no proof to this world and could only be accepted in faith.

Unresolved and hardly touched upon in the Old Testament is the mystery of death. Promises of restoration are all for this world and of this world. It seems that, for these amazing people, it was the future of the race that mattered, not the individual men and women of that race. Individuals die, are buried and live on in their children. 'The people whom the Lord has blessed' live on. The loss of the individual seemed to present no problem except that it made the believer passionately attached to the present life for it was only in the present life, the 'land of the living', that one had the companionship of God and could praise him.

> For Sheol cannot thank thee, death cannot praise thee; those who go down to the pit cannot hope for thy faithfulness. The living, the living, he thanks thee, as I do this day.[14]

Some faithful hearts knew better. Their hope went out from themselves, out from what they could see, from what they could understand, out from the accepted reli-

gious beliefs of their people, to a God who was faithful.
In fidelity of life, in humility and prayer they had some-
how met God and knew they were loved. God was their
friend. The bond of friendship was indestructible. God
would not let a friend down.

> Therefore my heart is glad, and my soul rejoices; my
> body also dwells secure. For thou dost not give me up to
> Sheol, or let thy godly one see the pit. Thou dost show
> me the path of life, in thy presence is fulness of joy, in
> thy right hand are pleasures for evermore.[15]

And:

> If I ascend to heaven, thou art there! If I make my bed in
> Sheol, thou art there.[16]

In his book, *Being as Communion*, John Zizioulas, the
Orthodox theologian, contends that we owe our concept
of person as unique and irreplaceable to Christianity
alone.[17] The concept emerged as the early Greek fathers
struggled to understand who Jesus was and the Father
from whom he derived. 'Person' became the key concept.
It is the development of personhood that alters the view
on death. Death is tragic and unacceptable only when we
are conceived as persons, of unique identity.

> As a biological event death is something natural
> and welcome, because only in this way is life
> perpetuated . . . [18]

Perpetuated because the survival of the species.

> The life of God is eternal because it is personal, that is to
> say, it is realised as an expression of free communion, as
> love. Life and love are identified in the person: the

28

person does not die only because it is loved and loves;
outside the communion of love the person loses its
uniqueness and becomes a 'being' like other beings, a
'thing' without absolute identity and 'name', without a
face. Death for a person means ceasing to love and to be
loved, ceasing to be unique and unrepeatable . . . The
eternal survival of the person as a unique, unrepeatable
and free hypostasis as loving and being love, constitutes
the quintessence of salvation, the bringing of the Gospel
to man. In the language of the Father, it is called
'divinisation' which means participation, not in the
nature or substance of God, but in God's personal
existence. The goal of salvation is that the personal life
which is realised in God should also be realised on the
level of human existence.[19]

People who could pray

O God, thou art my God, I seek thee, my soul thirsts
for thee; my flesh faints for thee, as in a dry and weary
land where no water is . . . thy steadfast love is better
than life . . . [20]

implicitly know that such love is indestructible and will
prove stronger than death. From the midst of the whirl-
wind God gave Job his answer:

I am God, you are a human being. Where were you
when I laid the foundations of the earth . . . did you hear
the morning stars singing and the mysterious heavenly
beings shouting for joy? Had you anything to do with
the curbing of the seas, marking out the bounds they may
not pass? Can you lift up your voice to the clouds, that a
flood of water may cover you? The secret ways of
animals, dusk and nightfall, the teeming life of this
wonderful creation, all goes on without you, Job.[21]

Job is silenced in the awareness of his insignificance and ignorance. 'I am God.' This is the only answer there can be; but, whereas the people of old had only their own hearts to assure them, we have an authoritative answer to the burning questions: What is God really like? Does God love us? Does God love us beyond death?

What the people of old could only hope was true we know with certainty through Jesus Christ our Saviour, who abolished death and brought life and immortality through the gospel.[22]

The early Christians believed that all the unanswered questions inherent in the Old Testament find their answer in Jesus, all the hopes and promises their fulfilment.

3

Faith itself is a mystery. Why is it that some people are able to believe and others not? That those who have never heard of Jesus – and those whose Christian education has been so meagre, so distorted that they too can be said never to have heard – should not believe, is understandable. What of those, apparently sincere who, having examined the claims of Christianity, read the New Testament and still withhold belief? People can be exposed to the same influences, given the same teaching and perhaps only one or two of a group will give committed assent. The evangelist John brooded over this question. Though he rounds on some as deliberately refusing the light, choosing not to see because their self-interest is threatened, he realises that this is not always the case and he bows before the mystery. 'No one can come to me unless the Father who sent me draws him.'[1]

Matthew agrees with this, assigning Peter's confession of faith to 'my Father in heaven'. Faith, then, is not merely a human decision but a divine gift, given to some, withheld from others. I recoil from the implications of this. Can God have favourites? A god who gives gifts to some but arbitrarily denies them to others? This is not the Father of Jesus who, in Jesus, gives all there is to give. We would rightly deny our heart's allegiance to such a god. In Jesus we are sure that all is always love and ordained to love: gifts given, gifts witheld. This too we safely leave to that Wisdom whose driving energy is to make every single one of us completely happy.

31

One hears in the voice of Julian of Norwich the ring of conviction when she says:

> Our soul is so preciously loved of him that is highest, that it passeth the knowledge of all creatures, for there is no creature that is made that may fully know how much, how sweetly and how tenderly that our Maker loveth us.[2]

Divine love is so other that it escapes comprehension even though our earthly experience of love gives us the word wherewith to name it. There is one human creature who has known it to the full capacity of a human mind and heart, namely Jesus. All the gospels make clear his pressing awareness of the holy Mystery that he called Father. The evangelist John goes so far as to have Jesus claim that he sees the Father and that his self-identity derives from his awareness of being known and loved by God. 'I know him', the humble man asserts as he walks our earth, experiencing life in a fully human way.

For my part, I base my life on this certitude of Jesus, on the God he is sure he knows in the profound intimacy of union. My faith is the faith of Jesus, derived faith, so to speak. Without Jesus I could not believe. I might affirm some vague apprehension that the world is not meaningless and that maybe the mystery is holy Mystery and hopefully interested in us but I would have no assurance, no certainty. As it is, I claim no other knowledge of the divine Reality other than I find in him. He is for me the Star, the Light of my life. I know him to be the 'Beloved' and want to live my life listening to him.

The Christian understanding goes beyond the notion that Jesus was just a divinely inspired, divinely moved human being representing for us God's goodness and love. In Jesus, God's own self is given to us, nothing less. In Jesus' person we encounter the holy Mystery directly. To believe in Jesus is to believe in the Father and yet Jesus is not the Father. Long reflection on all they had seen and heard and their living experience of communion with the risen Jesus in the Spirit, brought the first witnesses to an understanding of the eternal plan of God, to a knowledge of God as a communion of love.

> For he has made known to us . . . the mystery of his will, according to his purpose which he set forth in Christ as a plan for the fulness of time, to unite all things in him, things in heaven and things on earth.[3]

John Zizioulas has expressed it another way:

> The being of God is a relational being. Without the concept of communion it would be impossible to speak of the being of God. The Holy Trinity is a primordial concept and not a notion which is added to the divine substance or rather which follows it . . . the substance of God, 'God', has no ontological content, no true being without communion.[4]

Just as no one can stand apart from the holy Mystery, neither can anyone not have to do with Jesus: every human person, just because a human person is a blood brother or sister of Jesus, is caught up into his life and destiny.

Primarily, I am sharing my experience with those who, like myself, humbly acknowledge with Paul and countless others that it has pleased the eternal Father to ' . . . reveal his Son to me.'[5]

This gift is never given for the recipient alone, it is given to one for all. We are entrusted with a treasure beyond price. What strikes us about Jesus as we meet him in the gospels is his tremendous awareness of what, in his person, was being offered to human beings.

Jesus reveals this in a parable. A man, seemingly by

33

accident, stumbles upon a treasure hidden in a field. He perceives its untold value and sets about securing its possession. He reburies it, hurries off and joyfully sells everything he has to buy the field.

To drive the message home, Jesus adds another story. This time it is a keen-eyed merchant, expert in detecting excellence, searching for precious pearls. His experienced eye alights on one – just one – and it is of such surpassing beauty, that he gets rid of everything else and in sheer delight buys that pearl. Jesus is depicting himself; his the perception, his the passion, his the joyful surrender of all to gain the ultimate prize.

I always keep in mind that what Jesus said and did came from his own experience. We must not think of him as the transmitter of an already written script of wise and holy sayings. Jesus lived our life in intimate union with his Father and always looking at God, constantly gaining experience and holy wisdom.

> Therefore I prayed and understanding was given me; . . . I preferred her to sceptres and thrones, and I accounted wealth as nothing in comparison with her. Neither did I liken to her any priceless gem, because all gold is but a little sand in her sight.[6]

As Jesus saw how things were and how accordingly human life was to be lived, so he showed to us not only by what he said but simply by being what he was and living as he did. We understand that Jesus himself is the embodiment of the wisdom that sits by God's throne

> . . . a reflection of eternal light, a spotless mirror of the working of God, and an image of his goodness.[7]

Jesus' life was a continual response of love to the Father who, he knew, loved him. Jesus called God his

Father; this title carried the richest implications for him. He knew well enough that, like every man and woman around him, he had been born of human ancestry. Biologically he was a Jewish male of such and such a family and a great deal could have been said about him by his acquaintances. But what we perceive is that Jesus' whole sense of identity derived from the relationship he knew he had with God. Of course, he was Jesus of Nazareth of Galilee, and he could point to his family, but his deepest reality derived from God's love for him. He understood himself only in relation to the God who was his Father.

Father implies self-donation. A father loves his child into being, endowing it with his own life. Jesus knew that he owed everything to the divine Fatherhood. God's self-giving love was the fount of his being and the whole movement of his heart was to give himself back in love. Obedience was the expression of this love-response.

> All things have been delivered to me by my Father; and no one knows the Son except the Father, and no one knows the Father except the Son and any one to whom the Son chooses to reveal him.[8]

The gospel of John elaborates on this theme of mutual love and knowledge. Knowing the Father's love for him, Jesus is aware of the Father's will that he is to be the first-born of many brothers and sisters; that he is to share his own relationship to his Father with us and he dedicates himself with unstinting generosity to this work. Both John and Paul saw deeply into this mystery of our identi-fication with Jesus, our sharing in his union of love with his Father.

If this divine vocation is, as with Jesus, our real identity, then our life's task must be to 'realise' it. We try to enter into Jesus' vision of life and see all things as illumined by

God's love. We are not mere individuals making our own isolated ascent to God alongside others. We are in communion, drawing life from a divine source. We are 'in' Jesus, borne along by him. Without him all that is truly permanently real about us ceases to exist. But it is a mistake to speak of our ascent to God. Divine Love comes down to us to take us up, and that makes a world of difference. Once again, it is a question of becoming what, by divine choice, we are: realising our potential, not effecting some weird metamorphosis.

We are entrusted with a truth of such magnitude and power that it can transform and bring to fulfilment the whole of creation as the 'kingdom of God': the truth that the Ultimate, the holy Mystery, is love. 'Communion is the nature of ultimate reality.'[9]

It is not enough to hold this notionally but in a way that transforms our whole existence. We have to work for a living faith. Unless we are fortunate enough to be supported by a community of faith, there is little in our culture to nurture a strong awareness of God. Religious truth tends to hover around the outskirts of our minds leaving great areas of our daily life uninfluenced. We must endeavour to bring it into the centre of our being. It has to be as operative spiritually speaking as our breathing. Breath exists only in the act of breathing and faith exists only when we are actually believing.

Faith is not and cannot be a possession, something we 'have' like a national identity or a university degree. I tend to think that one of our greatest weaknesses as Christians is to take it for granted that we 'have' faith and fail to realise how assiduously faith has to be activated. We would do well to take to ourselves the solemn injunction of Deuteronomy:

> Hear, O Israel: The Lord our God is one Lord; and thou shalt love the Lord thy God with all thine heart, and with

all thy soul, and with all thy might. And these words . . .
shall be in thy heart; and thou shalt teach them diligently
unto thy children, and shalt talk of them when thou
sittest in thine house, and when thou walkest by the way,
and when thou lie down, and when thou risest up.[10]

There can be no misunderstanding this text: the love of
God must be our absolute priority and this means we
reflect on it time and time again, punctuate our day with
remembrance of it. It would be a good thing to ask ourselves just how often, in fact, we do think about God's
love for us.

Whether we advert to it or not, all of us are seeking our
treasure, our heart's desire. If we want to know what we
reckon our treasure ask where our heart is. Around what
do our thoughts revolve? What is our preoccupation, the
underlying drive of our activity? 'For where your treasure
is, will your heart be also.'[11]

Deeper than our desires that are discernible, lies our
heart's yearning for its absolute Beloved. Our constant
seeking in spite of frustration, reveals that, implicitly at
least, we know that our heart's Beloved is somewhere.
Only Jesus had his heart absolutely in the right place all
the time. It is from him that we learn what it means to
live a life of love. Where else shall we find objective
knowledge of Jesus except in the scriptures?

I count myself fortunate that, from an early age, the
New Testament has been a living book for me. Maybe
here we have an instance of how God turns all to good.
My community at the time was impoverished in regard to
books, in part through lack of funds but also on principle.
Of course, objectively, this was regrettable but it did mean
that one was saved from dilettantism and obliged to make
the most of what was available. The scriptures, and in particular the New Testament, together with the missal and
breviary, were my pasturage, and so the New Testament

began to reveal itself to me. However, I know that there are serious-minded people who experience great difficulty with it and occasionally to such an extent that they stop trying and rely on other people's insights, receiving everything secondhand, so to speak. These texts come to us from antiquity and, like all ancient writings, do not easily yield up their full meaning. Whereas none of us feels obliged to master the intricacies of the Bhagavad-Gita, Sophocles or Ovid, as Christians we are obliged to expose ourselves to, and therefore come to grips with, sacred scripture. These writings are a divine gift, not a mere human achievement and, even though our untrained eye may fail to see their literary beauty, as Paul says, divine treasure is safest when concealed in an earthen pot lest we spend our time and attention admiring the vessel and fail to value the treasure, letting it spill away.

Today we have the benefit of wonderful biblical scholarship. Meticulous, conscientious, laborious research of dedicated men and women have made the scriptures accessible to us as never before and we can hardly plead excuse if we do not avail ourselves of their offerings. Granted, most people have neither time nor opportunity for a great deal of study, but a great deal of study is not the essential thing. I nearly always have a commentary at hand and read a little each day – more would be too much – and this takes me into deep water. I think the secret of 'success', though lies with our actual approach. We must not be casual in regard to scripture. It is sacred scripture and must be approached with the preparation, faith and reverence with which we approach all sacred things. These historical documents, truly human in that their authors' natural abilities and insights and – because they were human – limitations, contain revelation, hold within them the word of God.

The Christian Church has always acknowledged that, in a special way, the Holy Spirit used these writers to express and to preserve within the Church the truth of Jesus. We can call them the sacrament of the word of God.

The outward form of a sacrament may or may not appeal to our aesthetic sense, but it holds for us the reality of divine communication and, specifically, Jesus, risen and glorified as our saving Lord. Together with the Eucharist, with which it forms a whole, the Church esteems these writings her greatest treasure. In them we truly encounter and receive the divine Word who is Jesus. To disregard them would be to resemble the people who, invited to a wedding banquet and hearing the summons: 'Come, eat of the feast I have prepared for you', find something better to do. 'Where your treasure is there your heart will also be.' We are told: 'They made light of it.'

Whether we are about to listen as in the liturgy or read privately, we need to recollect ourselves and recall that this text contains a message of eternal life. We need to attend, be there, listen. I find that after fifty-five years of constant attention the content of scripture is inexhaustible.

We may have to lose the Jesus of our imagination in order to find the real Jesus. Like his first disciples, we too carry around with us prejudices that we fail to recognise, so deeply are they rooted, so much are they part of our inheritance. These prejudices arise for the most part from our desire to have Jesus as we want him, just as we want God to be a God that is amenable to us.

Like the disciples, then, we must undergo a conversion and allow our prejudices to be broken down – all the defences we have erected to protect ourselves from the reality of God that Jesus embodies. If we sustain this impact, our faith will be purified and strengthened. We shall begin to see and love what we see.

It is easy to get discouraged in our wrestling with

scripture. So often it can seem that we derive no fruit from our labour and that we might as well give up the struggle. At times like these it is well to recall the sacramental character of the text. Just as we do not assess the fruits of holy communion by sensible effects, so neither must we in regard to scripture. If we approach with faith and with an earnest desire to do our best, we can take for granted that we have received nourishment, that, in fact, we have received the Lord.

St John of the Cross has an apposite saying that comes to mind:

> . . . fruit that is sweet, delicious and lasting is gathered in country that is cold and dry.[12]

We must not give up when we find ourselves in a country that is cold and dry. God is infinite Beauty and Bliss and surely contemplation of God and our life with God should be the most delightful experience on earth? Theoretically, perhaps, we could say that this would indeed be appropriate and ideal, but in reality we cannot count on pleasure attending our spiritual activities. When it is there we are grateful and use it – when it is not there we must be every bit as faithful. Deprivation of pleasure can thus become proof of our love and the genuineness of our desire.

It would be sad indeed if we Christians were to go elsewhere for our intellectual knowledge of God rather than to Jesus. Nowhere else shall we find pure truth. What does it matter, if, from time to time or even for a great deal of time, scripture, for us, lacks emotional stimulation? I suggest that, if we really examine the matter, we shall find that always, or nearly always, the mind receives food; it is the feelings that are starved. Of course, we would all like to have insights that illumine the mind and uplift, rejoice the heart, but when this is not so we can still use the 'dull' light the mind has received and use it in our daily living. Jesus exhorts us to

> . . . take heed what you hear, the measure you give will be the measure you get, and still more will be given you.[13]

We shall receive from our hearing as much as we bring to it and the more we receive the more will be given. Prayer, longing, the willingness to take trouble, these will ensure that our hearts are open to the Holy Spirit dwelling within us.

From the gospel account of the Resurrection appearances, we see that the risen Lord was revealed only to disciples, to those acquainted with him and who, however falteringly, had wanted and tried to be true to him. We read that, 'their eyes were held so that they did not recognise him.' Jesus was really with them but they failed to 'see' him and, suddenly, they did. A word, some gesture, brought revelation.

I think this shows how important it is for us to hear and read the familiar text, even though it can sometimes appear a dead letter.

> The Holy Spirit will teach you everything. The Holy
> Spirit is with us always, inspiring us, teaching us
> how to live, keeping us within the radiance of holy
> Wisdom – Jesus. And not infrequently, in the midst of
> our daily tasks or in the face of some event, tragic or
> joyous, his words come to mind, for the Holy Spirit will
> call to mind all that I have said to you.[14]

Thus, the sacred Word shows us the meaning of what is happening and, through the happening, we understand more deeply the sacred Word and exclaim: 'Oh, this is what Jesus meant!'

I place all my trust in the promise that the Spirit of Truth is with us, in the Church, in the hearts of the 'faithful', the 'communion of saints', and this means in my own heart too. Each one of us is as truly Jesus' disciple as were those to whom the words were first addressed. Each one of us must listen to the sacred words with humility, trust and dedication of self. Each receives on behalf of all. It is within the 'communion' that the fullness of the Spirit is given and no limits are set save those of our own making.

4

No matter what our background knowledge of scripture, no matter what our technical grasp of the text, it will remain essentially closed to us without our personal involvement. We can study a piece of music, the various movements, how the composer has obtained this or that effect; we can learn about the various instruments rendering the score, their unique tonalities and the role they play; but it is only when we surrender ourselves to the music itself that we really hear it, receive it and in some way become one with it.

We have to listen to or read scripture with our heart and never as a detached observer. I myself am being addressed. I am that woman Jesus encounters at the well, I really am. I take her words as my own and allow Jesus' response to fill my heart so that I can cry out: 'Give me that living water that is yourself.' I am the blind man longing for sight, or so I think, until Jesus challenges me: 'Do you want to see?' Trembling, because I know I cannot grasp the full implications of seeing – what would life be like if I really saw? – I still cry: 'Yes, Lord, make me see.'

I am the prodigal returning home and I allow myself to be loved in all my shame and misery, allow the divine arms to enfold me. I am each one of those characters whom Jesus encounters; yes, there is in me that carping Pharisee, the mean older brother of the prodigal son. I hear myself rebuked by Jesus for my obtuseness, knowing that the glance of love will heal me.

The gospels were written in this way, so as to speak to

the Christian heart always 'today' – 'Jesus Christ yesterday, today and the same for ever.' Above all, it is in the Passion narrative that we are meant to find ourselves and oh, how painful this can be! During the liturgy of holy week, the Church in the dramatisation of the Passion story calls on us to take the part of the crowd. I am sure we all recoil from this, from crying out: 'Crucify him, crucify him!'; and, 'Not this man but Barabbas!' And yet, have we but once deliberately wounded another? And we have, in fact, cried: 'Crucify him, get rid of him, he offends me!' We identify to some extent with all the characters of the drama: the disciples who desert him; Peter who denies him; the crowd; the Pharisees; chief priests . . . and, to quote Faber's hymn:

> My weak self-love and guilty pride
> His Pilate and his Judas were.[1]

Make no mistake about it, to expose ourselves, to meet Jesus in the gospel, is to cry out from a stricken heart: 'I am sinful.'

There can be no satisfaction with oneself. It is of no consequence that one cannot point to a specific serious sin – a protected situation, outside influences, may well have saved us from such; the light from Jesus reveals our depths, uncovers our basic meanness and selfishness. The so-called 'righteous' need conversion just as much as the so-called 'transgressors'. Those who can, perhaps with justification, claim to have kept the commandments, and those who have broken every law under heaven! Confronted with the unconditional, self-outpouring love of God revealed in Jesus, the distinction disappears. All are sinners, all are loved with an eternal love.

Reading the gospels with my heart I find myself questioning: Do I yet believe? What does it really mean to believe, to be a true disciple, to leave all, to live for God alone? And I cry out: 'I do believe, but oh, do help my unbelief. Show me continually, give me the light I need.'

You see, we can never answer these questions about ourselves with any certainty. We can only hope and pray. In my heart of hearts I do not want an answer for that could mean I rely on myself in some way, whereas I believe that divine Love wants me to rely only on itself.

We can be so familiar with the texts that we no longer hear them. We have, for instance, listened to the parables year after year after year and we take for granted that we have got the message, there is nothing more to learn. But the parables, when delivered, shocked the audience, jolted them, challenged them to think and think deeply; the parables overturned, not illustrated, the audience's understanding of God.

We have to try to recapture that shocking element. We too must experience the word of God as

> . . . living and active, sharper than any two-edged sword, piercing to the division of soul and spirit, of joints and marrow, and discerning the thoughts and intentions of the heart.[2]

We each have our cherished notions of God. We cannot avoid this. As human beings we must always imagine and express ourselves even to ourselves in symbols: that is, in ideas. Even the most abstract rational idea remains an image. An image is not an idol but can easily become one. We know when it has become one when we cling to it tenaciously, will not let it go even when, perforce, it is shattered before our eyes. And our so-called faith lies shattered with it. Our part in our striving to know and love God is to purify as much as possible our image of God. What other way is there for us who believe in Jesus than to be always testing our God against his image and being willing to leave our own notion aside to embrace him? We can do this work and must do it but this is not to say that thus we achieve knowledge of God. This is pure gift, a communication of God's own self to us, and this communication alone can destroy our idols.

My long exposure to the gospels has brought me to the point where I perceive one message and one message only, namely, that our God, Jesus' God, is total, unconditional, love.

This is not obvious. A great deal is said in the New Testament about human behaviour and the impression could easily be that here we have treatises on Christian behaviour. There is no doubt that the writers themselves were, in fact, greatly concerned with conduct. They were drawing on the early tradition, both oral and written, concerning Jesus' words and deeds and, many decades later, drawing out the implications for their particular flock. But I am convinced that Jesus himself was not preoccupied with conduct, with giving a moral code. It is hard to think that, when hobnobbing with 'tax collectors and sinners', he spent the time telling them how to mend their ways in the manner of John the Baptist. Once he had met Jesus, it is the tax collector Zaccheus himself who knows what he must do and sets about doing it. Jesus was intent only on revealing the true character of God. Ravished himself, he was certain that, once human persons had glimpsed the pearl there would be no question of their response. Gladly, they would give their all; they would know the meaning of love and love in return. 'As the Father has loved me, so have I loved you.'[3]

The source of Jesus' love for us was his Father's love for him. Experiencing the glory of divine love in and through Jesus, we would not need to be told to love others.

> . . . and you have no need that any one should teach you.[4]

So, for the true followers of Jesus there is no law. The Spirit who has taken possession of their hearts is their law.

Thus, it is no longer a case of 'you shall not commit adultery'. The disciple knows that no human person may be used in any way whatsoever for selfish gratification but, rather, the disciple is always the servant of the other. The neighbour whom one must love is as extensive as is humanity. The disciple, having experienced the reality of forgiveness, can never withold it from another. A moral code is replaced by pure love which fulfils the whole law. 'By love's resistless urge compelled', Jesus strove against human blindness and hardness of heart, strove to master them with the vision of incomparable love. His own lovely presence was itself the message, his unconditional love for each and everyone.

I here share my personal approach to the gospel. Of course, it is not the only one but I can say that I find it for myself most fruitful. The evangelists are preaching Jesus, showing who and what he is for us, and we can never exhaust his significance. Nevertheless, Jesus himself was concerned only with the Father. Jesus' focus was 'the kingdom of God'. Jesus was aware with unshakeable certainty of his unique union with God and that it was the will of this adorable God that he should be a true brother to us, be our light, reveal divine love, communicate his own vision and draw us into his union with the Father. The kingdom of God means that God is allowed to be God, the God of every human heart, allowed to be limitless, overflowing, beatifying love for every person.

Jesus understood that in his own person divine love was bursting its banks, surging into the world to make it God's own world, a realm of perfect communion of love. I keep questioning the text: what is Jesus revealing here of how God is to us? There is nothing contrived about Jesus' communication. All he says to us, all he does is simply the effect of his knowing God. He is thus, acts thus because

God is thus and acts thus. Loving God as he did he could not be other than he was nor speak and act differently. What is God like? This is the question I ask of Jesus. I try to put aside preconceived ideas, try to expose myself defenceless to the text.

Can we stress enough how earnestly we need to pray, how ready we must be to be upset, 'cut to the heart', revealed in our terrible poverty; how we must allow for self-deception, for which we humans have an unlimited capacity? Have confidence: we are dealing with Love, a love that desires us and which will answer our sincere prayer and enable us to stand defenceless before Its Beauty; gradually, perhaps, for 'it would be too much for you now'.

It is the magnitude, the inconceivability, the sheer beauty that is our problem. In her commentary on Botticelli's painting, 'The Birth of Venus', Sister Wendy Beckett wrote:

> Venus comes naked, and this is the saddest part of the story: she is not permitted to step naked onto the land. . . . Flora holds out a glorious cloak to wrap around her. But she does so because our world is not strong enough to receive Beauty naked. When Venus steps into our world we shall cover her up, cover her with exquisite garments, hide away from us her pure radiance. Venus is Love as well as Beauty, the two deepest human realities. T. S. Eliot wrote that humankind cannot bear very much reality. Love in its nakedness and Beauty unadorned are too much for us.[5]

What is it about naked beauty and love that we find intolerable? For one thing, the contrast with ourselves is devastating. Any idea we cherish of our own spiritual beauty is destroyed. Moreover, such love and beauty are not manageable, we cannot get hold of them, cannot cope with them. They frighten us with their 'otherness', and at the least we tone them down to what we can endure, or, in our anger and fear, we try to exterminate them. This we did, of course, when the God of beauty and love came into our world.

In the gospels an occasion is recorded of three disciples receiving some mysterious intimation of the divine glory concealed in Jesus' lowly humanity. They were wholly ravished, taken out of themselves, and wanted to stay with it for ever. What else but beauty can so ravish the human heart? That people found Jesus beautiful, infinitely attractive, is beyond dispute. This was a beauty which could not be defined in physical terms. We are given no idea of what Jesus actually looked like. The beauty was one of personality, a spiritual quality. The people flocked to him, drawn as to a magnet, and hung upon his words.

> You are the fairest of the sons of men; grace is poured upon your lips.[6]

And they:

> . . . wondered at the gracious words which preceded out of his mouth.[7]

And again:

> No man ever spoke like this man![8]

Enchanted, people forgot their physical needs and failed to notice the passage of time. Jesus employed no rhetorical arts, no manipulative devices, but sat among the people as one of them, speaking 'as a man speaks to his friend', without condescension. He was simply sharing his own insight, seeing each one of them as the beloved of God whom God wanted to be completely happy in a

49

truly human way. He gave them recipes for such happiness, taught them how to pray to the One whom they could be sure loved them.

> In wisdom there is a spirit, intelligent and holy . . . lucid, spotless, clear, working no harm, loving what is good, eager, unhindered, beneficent, kindly towards humankind, steadfast, unerring, untouched by care, all-powerful, all-surveying, and permeating all intelligent, pure and delicate spirits.[9]

No spirit so delicate as his!

> . . . a breath of the power of God, and a pure emanation of the glory of the Almighty.[10]

And:

> With what can we compare the kingdom of God; or what parable shall we use for it?[11]

I believe that in the parables as Jesus first delivered them, some of our deepest religious questions and anxieties are addressed. They are easily lost sight of.

For all their fascination with Jesus, the people as a whole – although they seemed to listen – did not really hear him. Their poor, weary hearts found solace and refreshment in his compassionate, friendly presence, this prophet who had risen up among them. Hopes were stirred, horizons glimpsed: 'God has visited his people.' They heard what they wanted to hear and listened from the context of their own, basically earthly expectations. When it became clear that their expectations were not to be fulfilled, that Jesus' thoughts were not their thoughts and his ways not their ways, they rejected him.

John expresses this in a dramatic scene. The crowds

follow Jesus out into a 'desert place', enraptured by his presence and words. At the end of the day he alone pays attention to their physical needs and feeds them in a miraculous way. The significance of this 'sign', this 'manna in the desert', is not lost on the crowd and it evokes a surge of nationalistic passion and hope. Here is the king they have waited for, the fulfilment of all hopes! This is the one to restore the kingdom to Israel, to bring in the golden age, the end of hardship and poverty, the end of subjugation to a foreign power! They rush to make him king. Jesus fled, hid himself.

Later on, when emotions had cooled, he reappeared and the people sought him out. He challenged them openly with their earthly expectations. He offers himself indeed as their golden age, their true food, the fulfilment of all their needs, but on God's terms, not their own. He hints at the costliness of this giving, hints at a sacrificial death, in which they too must mysteriously share.

> After this many of his disciples drew back and no longer went about with him. [12]

And then Jesus

> . . . went about in Galilee; he would not go about in Judea, because the Jews sought to kill him.[13]

In the moment of transfiguration, the prophets Moses and Elijah, who appeared with Jesus in glory, spoke of his coming death. The ensuing narrative makes it very clear that this conversation was lost on the disciples. The beauty of God, reflected in the beauty of Jesus, so surpasses all our earthly conceptions of beauty, that it can become anathema to us. For it is the beauty of a totally selfless love; a love that keeps nothing whatsoever for self but pours it out for the other – the mystery of God's own self lived out in history as 'there is no greater love than this . . . '

We may not underestimate the enormous difficulty human beings have in accepting unconditional love, the love that gives all for nothing. We see the difficulty illustrated in the people Jesus encountered. Mark, the starkest of the gospel writers, has it that not one of them really understood. The people around, even those favourable to Jesus, could not but see him through old eyes; from a set, patterned mentality which could not allow for something absolutely new and breathtaking.

We fail also unless we make a special effort. We go on with our presuppositions, our hearsay about Jesus, the taken-for-granted 'truth' or 'truths of our religion', the common interpretation of Jesus' teaching, and therefore fail to hear, fail to see. The people did not see any real difference between Jesus and John the Baptist and there are writers today who declare that there is nothing that Jesus said that was not said 'of old'. He was another prophet in a long line of prophets – no small praise but, of course, totally inadequate.

Jesus knew he was new, unprecedented. That, in him, divine Love had burst through the floodgates and was let loose in the world; that if people would draw near, allow themselves to draw near, they too would be men and women of fire. Alas, human instinct is to hurry away and hide in the deep places of the earth from such wild love. Jesus knew that his coming opened an unending wedding feast – a joy that 'shall never be taken away from you', and this in spite of sorrow and woe. Guests at a wedding feast do not fast whilst the bridegroom is with them. Fasting is an age-long symbol of mourning, of repentance, of making reparation, of appeasing the wronged deity. It is a 'given' of almost every religion. It does not belong to Jesus' community, at least not with this significance. Jesus' disciples will certainly fast that others may eat; will certainly accept a discipline that sets them free from self-centred drives, but will not fast to obtain favours from God or anything suggestive of 'giving God something hard'. We must look carefully at our religious practices, the why and wherefore of them. Are they truly Christian? Is our attitude in undertaking them truly Christian? We are always in danger of succumbing to our non-faith, our inability to believe in God's unconditional love; always in danger of seeking ways of making ourselves secure from God instead of secure in God, our only security.

There is plenty of evidence in the New Testament itself that the earliest disciples experienced the same difficulty as ourselves in holding on to, at all times, the Truth, the only Truth – the self-communicating love of God – and falling back into ways of religious thinking and consequently practices (fasting for instance) that are not in accord with this Truth. The author of the letter to the Hebrews is concerned to urge his community not to resort, in their crisis of faith, to the supposed security of the temple sacrifices; priesthood, sacrifice, these have been fulfilled and hence abolished by the one completely adequate and effective priest who offered himself as the perfect sacrifice. Indeed, he goes on to encourage them to trust blindly in their great high priest, who has gone before them into the highest heavens, and to understand that they are utterly safe in him, anchored in him. Gone into the highest heavens, out of sight, beyond the range of our imagination, enfolded in Mystery!

The earliest disciples hoped for his speedy return and as year followed year with this expectation unfulfilled and they found themselves the object of petty and sometimes grievous persecution, they were bewildered. Things had not turned out as expected and faith wavered – or, is it more true to say, faith was showing itself to be charged with non-faith? The author is challenging his community to exert their faith. The Jesus he sets before them is the

53

one who knew the pain of being human from the inside. He is the 'pioneer of our faith', the one who showed us how to set our face steadfastly towards the 'promise', to gaze with blind trust on the holy Mystery even when it seemed blind and deaf to our woe. As the poignant words in Hebrews remind us, during his life on earth, Jesus petitioned God with loud cries and silent tears to deliver him out of death.[14]

These loud cries, and still more, these silent tears, were they reserved only for the 'hour of darkness', the climax in Gethsemane? Rather, did they punctuate his whole life?

Jesus' profound, unique knowledge of God, of the unspeakable ocean of love pent up in God, surely gave him also a unique insight into the truth of human beings. He saw us in our terrible reality of indigence and vulnerability, living far, far below what divine love intended for us and to which it was inviting us; alienated from this outstretched love instead of living in its embrace. He felt, as none of us ever can, our shocking selfishness, our blindness and the triviality which is its consequence. He saw the divine treasure bartered away for baubles, the holy pearls trampled upon. The sickness he encountered all around him, the mental disturbance, the deep fears and unhappiness, all these pierced his heart. This was not the divine will, the plan, eternal as the holy Mystery itself, to draw every man and woman into the safe haven of absolute security, peace, joy ('my peace', 'my joy') even whilst still confined in our pain-filled, 'unfulfilled', 'unsatisfactory' earthly life.

No one knows the Father except the Son. Jesus knew it to be his mission to reveal to us the true God, and this knowledge is the remedy for all our ills and is ultimately our perfect fulfilment. Men and women, throughout long ages, had formed images of God in their own likeness. The pitiful consequences of collective wrongdoing,

of the refusal to be faithful to their own nature, to see the
world as God's world and live in it on God's terms – these
consequences they attributed to God, reckoned them as
divine wrath and punishment. Such a God could not be
trusted to be generous and forgiving. Religion was a
system whereby this terrible God was held at bay. What
it must have meant to Jesus, all alive to the Reality, the
reality of total, unconditional Love! This was death, this
was what he prayed to be delivered from, for he found
himself immersed in it, in solidarity with us. Jesus was not
there to condemn but to save; before this intense misery
his heart knew only compassion. 'God made him sin for
us.' He had lived with us in the suffocating atmosphere
that alienation from God had created. Bombarded with
temptation even as we are, Jesus never succumbed, never
colluded with evil as we do, never ceased loving us. If he
pleaded to be delivered from death it was not so as to leave
us behind, but so that we could be taken with him out of
everything that was death-dealing. He shared our lot to
the full; this was his Father's will that he embraced with
all his heart.

As the author of Hebrews says: 'That is why he is not
ashamed to call them brethren . . . '[15] for he shared our
flesh and blood. And again: 'Here I am, and the children
God has given me.'[16]

In every possible way, by what he said, what he did,
what he was and, above all, by his unreserved gift of himself in dying – 'there is no greater love than this' – Jesus
showed the divine reality to be total Forgiveness, before
whom we could lay down our burden of fear, unsureness
and guilt. With such a God for our God we can afford to
forget ourselves in trustful living and selfless love of
others. 'Unselfishness is our greatest likeness to God.'
Human goodness is a consequence, not a cause, of the
holy Mystery's self-gift to us.

5

How familiar we are with Matthew's parable of the sower who went forth to sow his seed.[1] We could possibly recite it by heart. As we have it now it is heavily allegorised. Our attention is drawn thereby, from the joyful figure of the sower to the ground on which the seed falls: the exposed wayside where birds can feed unmolested, hard, stony ground, patches thick with thorns and thistles and, finally, good, productive soil. We are left in no uncertainty as to the interpretation, the allegory is explained in detail. The word of God can be heard by many different people, can fall like seed into countless hearts but often fails to bear fruit. The fault is not in the seed but in the ground it falls upon.

Jesus is sitting in a boat at the edge of the lake addressing the crowd. It is a rural setting and the image he uses is part of the people's workaday lives. Perhaps even as he talked he could point to a farmer in a distant field: the sight speaks to Jesus of his Father as, it seems, did everything about him, the world luminous to his loving, adoring eyes. Jesus' attention is on the sower and his uncalculating, indiscriminate scattering of seed, not on the places where it falls. Jesus had grown up in an agricultural community and year by year witnessed the miracle of tiny seed burgeoning into rich harvest: the actual superabundance of seed that nature provides and the incredible potentiality concealed within one tiny grain. The extravagance of nature, the superfluity of seed that trees and plants produce year after year spoke to him of his Father. 'The sower went out to sow'; we can see him striding along confidently, his purse bursting with grain, the supply is inexhaustible and so he can afford to be lavish, scattering seed around him as he goes along, not carefully watching that none gets wasted. Jesus wants to be like that, like his Father is, scattering handfuls of love abroad, giving himself without stint to human need. If this vision of Jesus and God is allowed to penetrate our minds and hearts, it will surely awaken a response: 'What must I do to receive such love as this? What God is giving must matter more to me than anything whatsoever. Show me how to respond! Help me!'

It is understandable that the early Christian teachers should use Matthew's parable effectively as an exhortation to moral responsibility before the demands of the gospel lest their communities 'receive the grace of God in vain'. Even so, we must admit that something has been lost. Our attention has been diverted from the picture Jesus gives us of God, to ourselves. Moralising has veiled the sheer beauty of Love. Very subtly, without our realising it and seemingly with the best of motives, by giving our attention first and foremost to our behaviour, we are shielding ourselves from the impact of God's love. We are confronted with a very infinity of love, one that literally surpasses our understanding and which threatens to overwhelm us. To a greater or lesser extent we turn away from the sheer mystery of Love to ourselves, to our 'service' of God, to what is manageable. Our conduct occupies the stage for we can, of course, do a lot about our conduct. Not for one moment must we underestimate the importance of conduct in our Christian discipleship but the point I want to make is that, unless we gaze and gaze on the God who really is, though our behaviour may appear impeccable it is hardly likely to be a response of love to Love. And that is what Love wants and only that.

Think of the parable Matthew gives us of a king who

threw a marriage feast for his son.[2] 'Marriage feast for his son', words that surely arouse a sense of joyful expectancy. The father–king prepares a banquet with which to honour his son: love for the son, love for the guests! Loaded table, waiting household and the joyful summons goes out: 'Everything is ready now (there is nothing more I can do), come to my feast! God, open house, loaded board, and everyone, literally everyone, the meanest riff-raff, welcome!' Love runs out all over the place, crying: 'Come to my feast!'

We need space to think of this, to allow the image of the father-king, of all that is implied about him, to sink into our hearts. We must not be quick to give our attention to the guest who is found at the feast without a wedding garment. Matthew, no doubt, found good cause to introduce this additional parable. We conjecture that there were some in his community that abused their status as Christians and gave scandal to others by their conduct. But we too are in danger of abusing it because not understanding unless we first give all our attention to Jesus. As the festive board bowed under Love's bounty, so must our hearts. We need to linger long on the picture of Love searching into every human haunt, 'gathering a people', everyone It can find, so that 'my house may be full'.

Do we Christians, I wonder, take seriously enough these verses from the gospels?

You have one master, the Christ.[3]

Jesus is Christ. Christ is Jesus, the human Jesus who is one of us. Philip's request, as we find in the gospel of John, is:

Lord! Show us the Father and we shall be satisfied.[4]

Jesus' answer is, in effect: 'Look at me. Go on looking at me.' John, illumined by the risen Lord, knows the absolute truth of 'to see me is to see my Father'. But the humble Jesus, held still within the limitations of mortality, did not say: 'Look at me', but, rather, 'Listen to me. I will tell you what the kingdom of God is like, I will tell you what it is like to know God's love and live as I do myself in that enfolding love.' The synoptic writers, just as much as John but in their own way are saying: 'Look at, listen to, this holy One.'

It is the spirit that gives life, the flesh is of no avail.[5]

This is true of the whole of our Christian existence. Our offerings of bread and wine remain merely our offerings of bread and wine, unless the Holy Spirit transforms them. So the words of scripture remain mere letters unless the same Spirit opens our hearts and vivifies the words that enter our minds, so that they too become bread of life for us. We take and eat the sacred Word, but it is the Spirit that ensures it is for us the living Word by which we live. This Holy Spirit is guaranteed; will

. . . teach you all things, and bring to your remembrance all that I have said to you.[6]

It is Jesus that the Spirit will reveal. Jesus is the revelation of divine reality. So, we must look and look, listen and listen and, by God's grace, understand and mould our lives in the light of that understanding.

We must never assume that we possess the truth. Truth must possess us. Truth is infinite. 'I am Truth', says Jesus. We enter into Truth by losing ourselves in the Mystery that is beyond our capacity. It is this exposure to Truth that brings us to holiness. Blinded by the vision of Truth, we cease observing ourselves, cease being interested in ourselves. Gladly, we will respond to every summons of love, for nothing else whatsoever will have the urgency to deflect us from hastening to the feast. The Holy Spirit, the divine Energy of the love of the Father for Jesus and of Jesus for his Father, will become divine Energy in us, transforming our minds and hearts into what we behold – not necessarily, and not most importantly, with our conscious mind, but in the secret region where is our true life and identity. We have to entrust ourselves in blindness and helplessness to divine Love. The seed God sows is God's own life; it holds within itself divine dynamism. How can it fail to grow if it falls into welcoming soil? The farmer, Jesus points out in another parable, is content to sow the seed and then wait patiently; there is nothing more that he can do. But, sure enough, there it is – the blade, the ear, the sheaf, the harvest home!

What of human conduct? Are we never to be told just what we must do? 'Listen', says Jesus, 'listen and listen until your heart understands, then you will know what to do.' The kingdom of God is not controllable and it can never be an achievement of ours.

None of us is consistent. We believe, partially, at this time, in these circumstances, but in all sorts of ways we reveal our lack of faith, our reverting to an image of God that does not bear the face of Jesus. It affects the way we live, the way we worship, approach the sacraments, our attitude to sin, to our neighbour, to our guidance of others. In fact, it conditions our view of life.

A particularly revealing criterion for a truly Christian mind is how we understand forgiveness of sin. Many of us have a deeply rooted conviction that sin must be atoned for – and by us. We must do penance for sin, perform certain religious acts, 'go to confession', for example, in order to put ourselves right with God, make ourselves acceptable before we can be admitted into the divine household. Whereas Jesus demonstrates so very clearly that this is not so. The Son is always at home in his Father's house. In Jesus, each one of us is always – no matter what we do – son or daughter in the home. This is what we must dare to believe and act on accordingly.

Whatever its etymology and the old usage of the prefix 'for', our word 'forgiveness', as it strikes the eye and ear, carries a weight of theology. Like the word 'atonement', it hits the nail on the head. It suggests something already given, there before the asking, as well as given for, given on behalf of. God is given in both senses: for us without our asking and so utterly for us. We can say that God is forgiveness; that is, God

> . . . was in Christ reconciling the world to himself, not counting their trespasses against them.[7]

A total amnesty is declared, unconditional forgiveness. All the writers of the New Testament proclaim this, it is the substance of the good news. It is the expression of divine Love's coming to meet us in the reality of our sinfulness.

What must this assurance of amnesty have meant to the ancient peoples? Almost of necessity they were religious, acknowledging a power outside themselves, a power to be feared, to whom they were answerable. There was little to assure them that they were in a safe relationship with a deity; that they stood blameless before it. Even the Jews were not exempt from this anxiety, as Paul, an observant Jew himself, so poignantly expresses. Their very law and the demands it made on them only highlighted their sinfulness and their inability to keep the law. It is clear that Paul is not referring merely to the externals of the Torah but its inner demands. He found himself helpless and he suffered a conflict between his natural selfishness and the light afforded to his spiritual self by the Torah. He was to describe himself as the greatest of sinners because he persecuted the Church. Paul was quite, quite sure that Jew as well as pagan stood before God as transgressors. Then in Jesus comes the incredible news, God does away with sin;

it is alright, absolutely alright! God reconciles you to God! What you cannot do God does in glad, costly love. God takes the burden.

We are never allowed to minimise sin as though it can be brushed away as dust off the shelf. But done away it is. Luke sums up the content of the gospel which must be preached throughout the world as 'repentance and for-giveness of sin'. The first words of the risen Jesus to his shamed and fearful disciples, in the gospel of John, is one of forgiveness.

In our word-imagery, forgiving is an act. God forgives us our sins – if we repent. There is the supposition that something changes God, causes God to do something. We do something first and then God acts: forgives. Is this correct? I think not. This taken-for-granted way of think-ing affects our faith-life more than we realise. It is based on our own limited view of forgiveness as we experience it among ourselves. We are our own model. Our eyes are on ourselves not on the only model, the perfect revelation of God, Jesus.

Not once in the gospels, according to my knowledge, is it stated that Jesus said: 'I forgive you your sins', and yet this is assumed. How often we hear it said that Jesus for-gave the sins of the sinful woman, for instance. The text invariably has Jesus make a statement: 'Your sins are for-given.' For me, this is profoundly significant. Once again, we must recall the truth that Jesus was listening to the Father, looking at him, and inevitably all that Jesus thought, said, did, mirrored, embodied how God is to us. 'I do only what I see the Father doing.' His confident statement: 'Your sins are forgiven', is derived simply from his awareness of divine Love's open house, open arms, unalloyed friendliness and acceptance; Its desire to receive us.

Jesus saw his Father as forgiveness. There was never a time when God was not forgiveness. God does not become forgiveness through any act of ours. Our repentance can mean only one thing, that we open our heart to the welcoming love of the Father. The woman 'who was a sinner' had experienced this truth before Jesus spoke. Jesus confirmed how things were. The woman had done nothing to 'get God to forgive her'; we presume that Jesus, through what he was, had touched her heart and enabled her to 'return', accept the proffered love of God. Nothing more was needed: her loving gesture, her outpoured tears were an expression of gratitude and love which Jesus acknowledged to be such. She loves greatly because she knows herself totally forgiven.

There is the well-known story of the paralytic lowered down by his friends through the roof in front of Jesus. Jesus sees their faith we are told: the faith of the friends and of the sick man himself (presumably he accepts their ministrations). This faith was probably nothing more than a trust that Jesus could help and his help was of God. It is not insignificant that the man was paralysed and not far-fetched to suggest that he was paralysed with fear and guilt, whether the guilt was justified or not. In this he represents our human condition. Only the sight of the loving, compassionate face of God, revealed in Jesus, can rid us of our bondage. Jesus here has double vision: he sees the face of his Father, he sees the torment of the poor man before him, and exclaims:

Take heart, my son . . . your sins are forgiven.[8]

The man is forgiven because God is forgiveness.

Jesus' God, the only God, is God-for-us, God given to us, God always turned to us, God there for us. The coming to Jesus, that movement of faith, is all that is needed. It is not that this faith turns God to us; faith is our walking into God's arms, or better, flinging ourselves into them. Relieved of his crushing burden, the paralytic, the one-time sufferer can get up, shoulder his bed and walk home.

This is the effect of every true 'sight' of God, not physical healing necessarily, but freedom from an intolerable burden of fear and guilt and the ability to live life to the full.

We shall notice how, in Matthew's gospel especially, though it features in the others too, preaching the good news is constantly linked with healing as though the one affected the other. Matthew gives a picture of Palestine as a vast hospital ward, so many times does he refer to the crowds of sick that were brought to Jesus for healing. We get the refrain:

> And he went about all Galilee, teaching in their
> synagogues and preaching the gospel of the kingdom
> and healing every disease and every infirmity among the
> people.[9]

And Jesus:

> . . . went up into the hills, and sat down there. And great
> crowds came to him, bringing with them the lame, the
> maimed, the blind, the dumb, and many others, and they
> put them at his feet and he healed them . . . [10]

Luke proclaims:

> I bring you good news of a great joy which will come to
> all the people.[11]

This news of great joy is the cure-all for all our spiritual ills and maybe for many related physical ones also. But we do not hear the news of great joy, do not see the wondrous sight. Our god is a god of our fashioning and this god lays heavy burdens on our backs; this god is one that reaps where he never sowed, a hard, relentless taskmaster, and our spirits lie broken under a great weight. Jesus sees all this and cries out:

> Come to me, all who labour and are heavy laden, and I will give you rest. Take my yoke upon you, and learn from me; for I am gentle and lowly in heart, and you will find rest for your souls. For my yoke is easy, and my burden is light.[12]

How often in the name of God, who is no true god, we lay intolerable burdens on others, even on little children. Instead of concentrating on showing them in one way and another, the tenderness, the compassion, the sheer friend-liness of God, we warn about sin and its consequences, insist on rules and regulations, and hearts turn away from such a god. The human heart refuses to take such a god seriously or else 'serves' God in fear, keeping every rule, clinging desperately to law and structures. If only each one of us would go to Jesus for a true picture of God! If only we prayed constantly:

> Let me see your face, let me hear your voice, for your voice is sweet, and your face is comely.[13]

Luke gives us a cluster of revealing stories. Jesus is scan-dalising the scribes and Pharisees by keeping company and eating with tax collectors and 'sinners', people excluded from the religious community. Jesus, a devout, observant Jew was doing the unthinkable and certainly the non-acceptable. He was violating the boundaries between those acceptable to God because of their obedi-ence to the law, and those who, breaking these laws, had set themselves 'outside the mercy'. There is no doubt that the parables addressed an historical situation but the underlying outlook and attitudes of those involved are universal and touch the deep centre of true religion and Jesus' message. As always, the all-important focus of the parables is God, what God is like, how God views us.

> For there is no distinction; since all have sinned and fall short of the glory of God.[14]

The shepherd, full of concern for the strayed sheep, taking it upon himself to look for it and bring it home; the housewife, searching for her precious coin and sweeping diligently until she finds it; the father of the prodigal running out to meet his homecoming son, and the joy in finding; all three characters tell us of God, of how God runs out to meet us, labours to find us, oblivious of the grief we have caused. We are shown how precious we are, what joy God has in us when we are at home, safe and trusting in love. The sheep, the coin, contribute nothing to their rescue and the prodigal's movement is minimal. It is the father who brings him home, in distinction to his just being around the place where he can eat, find shelter and survive. God is forgiveness. We have only to receive. No act of ours is needed to bring a change in the divine heart to induce it to turn to us in mercy.

I have lived with the unforgettable story of the forgiving father and his wastrel son for many long years and it is a story that has been commented on over and over again, understandably so. My own appreciation was deepened by Kenneth E. Bailey; in his book, *Poet and Peasant Through Peasant Eyes*, he writes:

> Two aspects of parabolic interpretation still need serious attention. These aspects are the cultural milieu and the literary structure of the parables . . . Significant elements of the cultural setting of the synoptic parables can be delineated more precisely through discussion with

contemporary peasants, through minute examination of Oriental versions of the Gospels, and by a careful study of pertinent literature.[15]

To do justice to the fruits of such an investigation would mean transcribing everything Bailey writes, so I must confine myself to the points that struck me most.

What emerges more emphatically than ever from the dialogue with Arab peasants and Oriental writings, is the father's love, its self-disregard and total generosity. The son has broken every conceivable law of filial piety: to demand his inheritance is tantamount to expressing the wish that his father were already dead. He could hardly have gone further in his contempt for his father, for his inheritance and for the larger community of which he is part. The father, insulted, wounded to the heart, remains steadfast in love, longing for his son's return.

Need brings the wastrel back, sheer desperation since now he has no other resources. His heart is not involved. There is as yet no recognition of the wrong he has done and he intends, not to crave forgiveness, no, but to ask for a job. Bailey has something to say here: a servant has independence, he gets a wage and has his rights, but a son lives in a different context, one of filial dependence where everything is received as gift from the father. The son shows a tiny scrap of confidence in his father's goodness in that he is quite sure that he will not be left without food or shelter. As for the father himself, all that matters is that the young man has come home, he is there to be loved.

The father, a venerable figure in the community, forgets his dignity, forgets convention and rushes out, runs to embrace the returning wanderer who is yet 'a great way off'. A patriarch does not run and most certainly does not take the initiative in reconciliation with a son who has wronged him so grievously and shown his contempt for the larger community. But this father does so, flings his arms around his loved one and kisses him. His action forestalls the response that custom demanded of the villagers. In no way would this sinner be allowed to walk freely into the community, accepted once again into full membership. The father's gesture disarms them. If the one most wronged receives him thus, how can they act other?

The son had thrown away his privileges; they meant nothing to him. All he valued was money and the freedom to be his own master and do what he liked. He has lost everything and is reduced to ruin. It never enters his head to imagine that everything would be restored. But it is. The plenitude of his father's love and forgiveness is expressed in act. The prodigal is clothed in the robe of sonship, the ring, symbol of trust, is put upon his finger, his feet are shod with sandals in token of his authority and there he stands before all: his father's son, heir of his house! As happens only for the most festive of occasions, the fatted calf is killed and all the village summoned to share in the father's overwhelming joy. 'Can you see,' Jesus is saying to his critical audience, 'this is what I am doing and I am doing only what I see my Father doing?'

The amazing thing is that there is no question of the son having first to make reparation, prove his repentance. This would have been the normal procedure. Nothing whatsoever is asked of him except to receive his father's love. This should give us pause and a nudge to look at our own deep-seated attitude regarding doing penance for sin. If we 'do penance for sin', we are doing it in our own name, not in the name of Jesus. For Jesus, repentance simply means walking into God's arms and allowing ourselves to be 'kissed better'. Can we believe this? We see in the story that it is the embrace, the kiss, the unbelievable acceptance of the father that made the sinner better. It was this that really changed his heart.

Let us imagine what happens when the feasting is over and the door closes behind the guests. No stretch of imagination is called for, no flights of fancy. From being a starving outcast with the bitter knowledge that his misfortunes were his own doing, the prodigal finds himself once again the cherished son, at home in his father's house. At home? Would he feel at home? Hardly. For one thing, no tenderness on his father's part, no encouragement from the rest of the household, can spare him the pain of awareness of what he has done. The more he experiences his father's generosity, the more he knows his father, the more acute his sorrow and shame. Will he ever forget the cruelty of the wound he inflicted on his father? There can be no escape from this pain whilst he stays at home. What is more, the years away have coarsened him and this he realises. He feels he is unfit to be in the family home, close to his father. For all the love the latter shows him, the son experiences estrangement. He lives in another world from that of his father; their interests, their values are different. The temptation to run away from it all could be great, yet the finest proof the son can give of his gratitude, and desire to love and be a true son, is to stay at home, receive all the father gives him, endure his presence. Gradually, he will be purified and transformed. Living with his father he will become like his father; he will become what he is – son.

We see from this story how divine Love is the 'given': unconditional, absolute. All else is drawn into this magnetic field. Divine Love draws, empowers, purifies, transforms. This is the Christian understanding of repentance and atonement.

There is another character in this inspired story – the first-born. Here Jesus addresses his critics directly: the 'righteous' who are indignant at his 'receiving' sinners and eating with them. We must not overlook the concern, the tenderness with which Jesus appeals to them. To all appearances, the elder son remains dutiful. Bailey, leaning on Oriental custom, asks why he did not, as the eldest, react to the younger man's outrageous treatment of the father, but perhaps this is pushing the parable too far. He is out in the fields when the prodigal returns and learns of the homecoming from a servant whom he questions as to the sound of revelry. 'Your brother has come and your father has killed the fatted calf so glad is he to have him home.'

Instead of delight, instead of hastening in to share his father's joy and take his place at his father's side, the elder son is furious and refuses to attend the feast, thus insulting his father. Once again, we see the father totally disregarding this aspect, concerned only for this elder son he loves. He leaves the gathering – ignoring convention – and comes to plead with his son. How sharp a contrast!

'For all these years I have served you. And I never disobeyed your commands; yet you never gave me a kid that I might make merry with my friends.'

The son's talk is of service, of a gift now and then, of 'his' – not 'our' – friends, whereas for the father it is: 'My son, beloved, everything I have is yours. You are always with me. Between you and me there is no mine or yours!'

For the son it is 'that son of yours', for the father 'your brother'.

The younger man allowed himself to receive his father's love and change. Will the elder? Neither son, for all their association with him, knew the father. They were sons only in name. It was the younger, the wastrel, who, in the end, proved most open. Destitution, failure, did what prosperity did not do. In actual fact, it was those who had failed, who were aware of their need who listened most readily to Jesus, whereas the 'righteous', the 'obedient' were closed. We discern, too, I think, how God dislikes the idea of 'service', of our being 'servant'. God wants us

as sons and daughters, children of the home. 'I do not call
you servants but my friends', says Jesus.

Every serious–minded Christian knows that he or she
falls short. Even leaving aside the word 'sin', we are aware
of much selfishness in our thoughts and actions. The only
way to deal with this is to see it all against the background
of divine Love and divine forgiveness.

Our actual perceived shortcomings apart, those things
which call for genuine sorrow, many of us seem to have
an innate sense of guilt and fear that has little to do with
actual consciousness of sin committed. It is insidious and
works underground in all sorts of neurosis, spiritual aber-
rations, dreadful images of God and general unhappiness.
We seem to feel guilty at the reality of our humanity. We
do not want to be human and are ashamed of being
human! We have an illusory notion of what we ought to
be like, of how fine a creature the ideal human being is,
and we are torn with guilt because we do not fit this
image. An accusing finger is pointed at us. Whose? Not
God's certainly, not Jesus' God. It is the finger of our own
self–condemnation and I think we have to say a collective
condemnation.

We are not born into a vacuum but into a human society, into a culture whose ways of thinking, whose
consciousness of reality we instinctively imbibe. Haunting
us, no matter how we try to suppress it, is the sense of
emptiness, of nothingness. Normally we deal with it and
much of the time, perhaps, it does not trouble us, not
consciously, but every now and then it raises its frighten-
ing head, or heads – for it takes various forms. We feel
guilty that we are weak, dependent and needy, that, in
fact, we are not splendidly self-sufficient; that we feel
unfulfilled, incomplete; that we suffer from temptations
and have within us forces of which we are afraid. In short,
we are aware of how little we belong to ourselves, how
little we possess ourselves in spite of our passionate desire

to do so. We are held fast in the oppressing embrace of a feeling that we are to blame for this. Things should be otherwise for us and somewhere we are falling short and are guilty.

In reality, the source of our supposed guilt is our trea-sure – our humanity. True, this humanity is flawed by sin but, because of Jesus' victory, need not be subject to sin. When Paul says that Jesus was born a subject of the law to redeem those subject to the law (that is, ourselves), what he means is that Jesus, though 'rich' in himself in that in his deepest reality he was 'in the form of God' and beyond the contingencies and limitations of our finite existence, nevertheless became 'poor' for our sakes so that we might become 'rich'. He 'emptied' himself, became like us, subject to the 'principalities and powers'. The ancients personalised what they experienced as the press of temptation and their own helplessness before so many factors both within themselves and in the world around them. They believed that they were indeed subject to superhuman forces that controlled their lives. Paul is saying that, through Jesus' 'obedience' to these very powers – even unto what seemed their total domination in death – he set us free.

This does not mean that we should experience our-selves as 'rich', triumphant, lords of the world, free from the pitifulness of our human condition, but that this very 'poverty' of ours is now a 'clean' emptiness for God to fill with divine fullness. Our total 'obedience', with Jesus to our human lot is our surrender to God; it is sharing in the death of Jesus but a death that is all the time blossoming in divine life.

If we truly want God to be 'my God', 'my All', then we must accept the humanity that is the capacity for this God. Our innate illusion and the source of our guilt, fear and unhappiness, is that we can be our own good, our own completion and happiness. 'You shall be as gods.'

72

This inspired sentence exposes the root of all our illusion and unhappiness. It is our human dignity, our human glory to be the creature that can freely, with all the passion and energy of its being, proclaim God as God, 'One God', and open itself to receive the immensity of Love and surrender to It, joyfully discarding pretensions to finite, self-engineered, self-procured happiness.

If both the 'righteous' and 'sinners' stand on equal terms for entering the kingdom of God – that is, neither has a right, neither qualifies, to both it must come as free gift – what is the point of religious fidelity, of the practice of virtue, of trying to be good? From the gospel accounts it seems as if the 'sinners', in fact, get a better deal. What is the relation between good works and the kingdom of God? This question and the tension it creates teased the first disciples just as it teases us. It is important to disclaim any right to make the distinction 'righteous', 'sinner'. Even in Jesus' time, all that could be said with certainty of the 'sinners' who came to him was that they had broken social and religious laws. It is impossible to go further. If Jesus was explicit regarding the prostitute who washed his feet with tears and wiped them with her hair, that 'her many sins are forgiven her . . . ', he could have said this to any disciple, regardless of whether they had transgressed in an obvious way or not. We all have sinned. We all fall short of what is ordained for us and everyone needs forgiveness. We can never make a judgment that this one is a greater sinner than that one; this one more righteous.

6

We know the story well.

> For the kingdom of heaven is like a householder who
> went out early in the morning to hire labourers for his
> vineyard.[1]

A fair bargain is struck with the first batch of workers.
The owner of the vineyard tells them: 'Do a good day's
work for me and I will give you this amount of money as
your wages.' Employer and employees meet on equal
terms, each needs the other. Later in the day the owner
looks for more hands to help with the harvesting. With
these labourers there is no bargaining but they go into the
vineyard with the master's promise of a fair wage. Again
and again he goes out to collect further workers with the
same assurance of fair returns until the very end of the
day. At the last hour he notices loiterers in the market-
place and asks them what they are doing there and why
they are not at work.

'No one has hired us', they answer.

'Get you into my vineyard', is the peremptory reply.
Bargaining is out of the question in this instance and, we
note, the master gives no promise of payment. These poor
fellows go into the vineyard to do what they can do at the
last lap, trusting only in the goodness of the one who had
bothered to notice them.

The moment of truth comes at the end of the day
when the owner of the vineyard summons the workers to

receive their pay. He begins with the last to come, those who had hardly done any work at all, and they receive a denarius, the wage bargained for and agreed upon with the first batch of labourers as a fair wage for a day's work. Seeing a denarius in their palms, the latecomers would know that this was no wage but pure gift. Each of the hired men, whatever the hours they had put in, received no more and no less than a denarius. The first to come, those who had indeed slogged all day long, looked on, it seems, with equanimity. They did not begrudge such generosity for, of course, having deserved infinitely more than these others, they would get a handsome bonus. They did not. They too received one denarius, and burst out in bitter resentment.

'Take what is yours', is the owner's chilly response. From first to last theirs has been a business transaction. They have nothing to complain of, they have received what was promised. With the others, in varying degrees, there had been trust in the owner's goodwill. They had gone into work without assurances. The wage they received bore no relation to their labour. The system of merit and reward was overthrown.

This is what the kingdom of God is like, Jesus is saying. It is the rule of one who gives all for nothing. We are meant to be shocked by the injustice of this parable. Is what it is saying really true? Does God give everything for nothing? Does not this contradict a whole tradition of ascetic discipline and of human effort if we are to reach our 'heavenly reward'? Is not the path to God thorny and laborious? 'Narrow is the gate and straight is the way that leads to life.' God gives everything for nothing? 'Yes', says Jesus.

I think we miss the point if we interpret the resentment of the conscientious, hard-working men who have put in the full time of labour in the scorching heat, as petty exclusiveness. In its original context, insofar as it comes

75

from Jesus, this parable reflects his attitude to the out-
siders, the 'sinners', those who, it seems, had flouted the
law, had not borne the burden of faithful, costly obser-
vance. At a later stage, used by the early Christian
teachers, the context would have shifted to the acceptance
of Gentiles or pagans into the Christian fold without the
obligation to undertake the full weight of Jewish law and
ritual.

A deep impulse of our human nature is violated. Jesus
is aware of this. Over and over again, in one way or
another, he has endeavoured to show that something very
radical in our nature has to be denied if we are to enter
into the kingdom, have the outlook, the mind, of God.

Jesus is not being difficult, refusing to explain things
clearly when he could do so. Once again, we are looking
into the well of Mystery. We are being confronted by a
God we cannot comprehend and, of course, we flounder.
We long for certainty regarding our service of God. We
long to have the assurance that we are good, that our lives
are meritorious and that we can offer plentiful gifts to
God, and if we were to uncover the underlying motiva-
tion, I think we would perceive that it is to make sure
God will love us and reward us. We are wanting to 'be
pleasing to God' because of our own goodness. Perhaps
we would discover that we are intensely preoccupied with
our self-image and, in fact, far more concerned with
seeing ourselves as good than in being good! Jesus is
telling us that it is possible to live a devout religious life –
'all these years I have served you!' – and, yes, truly bear
the burden of the day and the scorching heat, but for ourselves, our eyes are not on God but on our virtue, our
good works, our own goodness.

However, as we have already seen, the moral implications are not the first concern of Jesus; he is trying to tell
us what his Father is like and how his Father sees and deals
with us. As we see from the gospel accounts, it was the

'righteous', those who took their religious obligations seriously, who had the biggest difficulty in accepting Jesus' message, that God's love can never be earned but is bestowed in complete freedom. At the same time there is nothing whatever to suggest that Jesus tells us to sit back and take it easy. The historical context of Jesus is a religious one and he assumes the keeping of the commandments and moral striving. His unhesitating response to the question, 'What must I do to inherit eternal life?', is 'Keep the commandments.' To the woman taken in adultery whom he refuses to judge, and allows no one else to judge, he enjoins: 'Sin no more.'

Jesus was himself an example of human goodness, but with him it was a pure response to love, a pure desire to do the will of his Father whom he loved, to devote himself to his Father's purpose. Jesus was not interested in himself, in his own perfection; he was not nurturing an image of himself as a holy man. He disregarded how others saw him and out of love for his Father and for a poor fellow human, stepped outside the law and was counted a sinner. Without any doubt, at the time of his death, his public image was that of a felon.

> Before you can see what you cannot see, you must
> believe it. Walk on in faith until you reach the point
> where you can see.[2]

I believe that a living grasp of Jesus' meaning – and that means one that influences our whole life – is properly a mystical grace, something the Holy Spirit must work in us. No amount of thinking about it, no conceptual knowledge can elicit it. But what we can do is ponder over and over again the reality of God's freely given love, as Jesus shows it to us, try to base our lives on this love, hold firmly to the truth that we are in the Father's house, already loved with no need to prove ourselves, no need to merit an entrance into that hearth, home and heart. It is all ours by gift.

What is asked of us is that we should live as a loved child lives, doing always what pleases the parent. In this way we can give up the anxious fretting to be sure – sure that we are doing 'right', that our motives are pure, and so forth. We cannot know these things and there is no need to know. Rather, it is best that we do not know. If we had the surety we crave, we would be relying on ourselves, not leaning totally on the freely-given love of God. Yes, we do have to bear the burden of the day and the scorching heat when God so ordains, but not to merit, to earn a wage, not to give ourselves the satisfaction that we have indeed been generous, but work with our eyes closed, so to speak, because by doing do we are in some way opening ourselves and the whole world to God's love. The more light we have the less likely we are to claim that 'for all these years I have served you.'[3]

If we have reflected carefully on Matthew, where Jesus draws out the implications of the commandments,[4] in no way would we claim 'all these I have kept from my youth'. Our nature resents this spiritual inadequacy and we can, if we wish, choose not to see beyond our natural sight, set a level of virtue for ourselves that lies within our own compass and so remain complacent. We can choose illusion. We long to work as equal partners with God and we do not want something for nothing because then we would have no guarantee that we would get it. We can rely on our own reliability but not on God's! We like to feel sure that, if we have done our duty well, kept the law, lived to the best of our lights, everything must be alright. Justice is satisfied; not even God can ask more. God owes it to us to see that we get a just reward!

Divine Love knocks at our defended heart; the Strong One attempts to break in but we can be so set about with our securities that he withdraws defeated. Like Jesus' contemporaries, we do not want to feel the ground shift beneath our feet. We do not want to admit that we need a new orientation. Behind all this is our dread of uncertainty, our dread of mystery. We want to be told exactly what is right and what is wrong, what we must do and what we must avoid. We want authoritative assurances. If we do not find them within ourselves we hope to get them from someone else. But no one can give us the certainties we crave. We already have the only certainty there is and the only one we need, an absolute Guarantor of love and fidelity and it is by this Holy One we must live in peace and security.

Our fears, our yearnings for assurance, reveal clearly that we do not believe in God's unconditional love. If we really do believe then we can live happily without certainties, with no anxieties about failures. Jesus told a story that illustrates God's way of looking at us and the only appropriate response on our part.[5]

A man is going on a journey and, sending for his three servants, entrusts each with a sum of money with which to trade during his absence. The first two servants do exactly that and their investments yield good returns. The third servant is cautious. He is not prepared to take risks and buries his money so as to be quite certain that it is intact when his master returns. The first two servants receive hearty congratulations and are summoned in to joyful fellowship with their master. The third servant, handing over his unproductive sum, is treated with severity. The point of the story is, once again, the character of the master. The first two servants reveal it by their spontaneous trust. They know him as he is and act confidently. The thought of failing does not worry them. What if they do fail? Their master will know they have done their best and in no way will he reproach them. Confidence is mutual. It was this trust that delighted the master. Whereas, 'I knew you to be a hard man,' whines the third servant, 'reaping where you do not sow, and gathering where you do not winnow; so I was afraid . . . '

Can we say that there is nothing of this attitude in us, prompting our anxieties, our dread of not being certain? Are we so afraid of 'offending God', of committing sin, of failing in some way that we hardly live?

The same message is given in what is perhaps a more startling story.[6]

An employer discovers that his steward has been cooking the books and gives him notice. The steward has to think out what to do, how he is to support himself in the future now that his means of livelihood has been taken away. He devises a scheme. He curries favour with his master's debtors by a last use of his authority, remitting a great part of their debts. The strange thing is that the master, when he hears of what has been done in his name and why, instead of falling into a rage, commends the dishonest fellow for his astuteness. It is, again, Kenneth Bailey who gives me the key to this story. The astuteness lay in the steward's banking on the character of his master. He knew quite well that the orders would not be countermanded but the huge concessions honoured. The ruse had worked; the steward's future is assured and all because he recognised and relied on the generosity of his employer. 'I wish the children of light were as wise as that,' Jesus commented. 'I wish they would stake all; their life, their future on the goodness of God.'[7]

Jesus seems to imply that the steward's rascality faded into insignificance set against the tribute paid therein to his master's generous character. Is it not to say that we can give God nothing more pleasing than our trust in God's goodness and that this trust drowns our faults and failings?

Until we come to real faith, until we entrust ourselves to God's love, believe that we live already in the family home and have no need to force a way in by good deeds, we shall never know real peace of heart and never come to deep intimacy with God. We can have a splendid spiritual life which is, at bottom, no more than self-interest invested in spiritual shares. A loving intimacy means that all the attention is on the Beloved and not on the self, not even on examining whether the relationship is real, whether our love is really love. Jesus shows us how to live a life of love, a life wholly turned to the Father. We fix our eyes on him.

Jesus himself lived in human uncertainty. No blueprint was given him and he had to go by a strange, unknown way. He could not have foreseen the glorious consummation, the surpassing reward. Jesus walked into Mystery that became unutterably dark and painful but with the absolute conviction that it was Love. One thing became clear and that was that he must die and die cruelly. What is more unknown than death, being dead? For us, because Jesus went through it, the 'unknown' is now, in some sort, known: we know it to be the gateway into inconceivable bliss. Jesus had to surrender to the unknown as totally unknown, but anchored to the one certainty of his life, his Father's love. His Father could be relied on to save him ultimately, but when or how he could not know and, it seems, at the end, all felt conviction was denied him.

Truly he had to surrender to Mystery that was 'cloud and darkness' and unspeakable pain. With Jesus, our pioneer, we must consent to move in to the unknown, into what we do not understand, what upsets our calculations, our hopes, how we had conceived things should be. We must let go on our clutchings at tokens, our tenacious control of the shaping of our lives and walk trustingly as a loved child into the holy Mystery, unshod, with nothing in our hands. With his truly mystical understanding, Karl Rahner has written:

> Where hope is achieved as the radical self submission to
> the absolute and uncontrollable, there alone do we truly

understand, what, or better, who, God is. God is that
which of its very existence empowers us to make the
radical self-commitment to the absolute uncontrollable in
the act of knowledge and love.[8]

It is God who calls, God who empowers, God who
achieves. Everything is there for us – open house, loaded
board. Did it cost nothing? It cost God everything.
Scripture tells us so: the open house is a broken heart. So
deep, so awesome is the Mystery that I hesitate to make a
single reflection of my own. God's Mystery, is

> Christ in whom are hid all the treasures of wisdom and
> knowledge.[9]

Christ is the crucified One. The crucified Jesus is the
human image of the Mystery of Love giving itself to us.

> God was in Christ reconciling the world to himself.[10]

God gave all God had to give in giving us Jesus. God kept
nothing back from us, not even God's only Son, and in
this gift of Jesus is the gift of the divine Self. These are
scriptural expressions touching on the 'mystery hidden
through generations' and revealed only in Jesus, of how
God loves us, how total is the divine self-gift to each one
of us – and the cost.

> Jesus Christ is God's 'Beyond Self'.[11]

I shrink from further scrutiny of the Mystery of God's
'suffering'. It is truly most awful. I recall Walter
Brueggemann's allusion to God's grief in his Old
Testament studies.

> Jeremiah keeps listening. He dares to think he hears God

cry – with tears like fountains, eyes that run like aqueducts.[12]

However, I do not think the emphasis is on suffering but on that mysterious notion of self-emptying. We find it said of Christ Jesus that he 'emptied himself'[13] and even here we may not forget that Jesus is the human translation of how God is to and for us. It is the mystery of being 'Beyond Self', out of one's own possession 'in' the Other; the mystery of Love which is ecstatic. We are stammering about a gift of self to us that is absolute.

The burden of our reconciliation, our being brought home, is borne by God and joyfully. As prodigals, safe in the family home, we never forget this and try to respond with tender gratitude and eager desire to surrender to whatever the Father wills. Living with God we become like God and thus grow into our true identity. We must become who we truly are. Jesus was always Son, always beloved and, unlike the rest of us, never less than he ought to be. Nevertheless, like all human beings he was subject to the law of human development. He had to become more fully who he really was. It is the author of the Letter to the Hebrews who expresses this most forcibly:

> But we see Jesus, who for a little while was made lower than the angels . . . It was fitting that he, for whom and by whom all things exist, in bringing many sons to glory, should make the pioneer of their salvation perfect through suffering.[14]

Jesus himself had to be made perfect and through suffering. He had to grow into his vocation as great High Priest, the Christ, and it was by way of sharing fully in our human condition.

Although he was a Son, he learned obedience through
what he suffered; and being made perfect he became the
source of eternal salvation to all who obey him . . . [15]

In Harry Guest's poem:

The makeshift Tree became stained this time
With the red knowledge of obedience . . .
All that we dread unshirked and undergone.[16]

Jesus learned obedience through suffering. This simple
statement always makes me catch my breath. Can we ever
plumb its depths? It seems to me that we are being told
that Jesus, God's holy Son, had to experience the depths
of the human vocation. It is a vocation, a call that takes us
beyond human capacity, and can cut across nature's
course, and calls for a dying. The vocation to union with
the divine is experienced as a death to what is merely of
this world. It involves an emptying out of all that is not
God. This human being who was perfect Son had, nevertheless, to die to everything that seemed to make him
human. Jesus was the Word, God's utterance of the divine
Reality, God's expression of the divine Self in the world
as it is. By his loyal obedience, even to the death of cru-
cifixion, Jesus lived and showed what he was, God's
Truth. Jesus was always 'Yes', to God's self-giving to the
world.

We can think of Jesus' obedience as involving two
aspects. They can be separated only logically for in reality
they intertwine continually. First, there is love without
limit, love to the end, for us. His human heart had to
carry the immensity of divine Love. If Paul could say,
'The love of Christ drives me on', how much more could
Jesus say, 'The Father's love drives me on.' Secondly, Jesus
had to surrender to the mysterious, hidden work of God
to bring him fully to Sonship. We see that this action,

viewed from a human standpoint, seemed to demand a denial of who he was, a diminishment, a destruction. 'He emptied himself . . . '

The early Christians had enormous difficulty in coming to terms with the 'descent' of the Messiah into such appalling depths of humiliation and suffering. Not even their experience of the risen One could exorcise their bewilderment and horror. Both aspects of obedience must find their counterpart in our lives too. We can distinguish – artificially – between what we try to do and what God does in us. We can speak of active charity and of prayer, for the essence of prayer is simply allowing God to work in us, to bring us to perfect relationship with God. We are destined to share a bliss that is divine. 'Having joy set before him, he endured the cross and its shame.'

We cling to our pioneer, our brother, our great High Priest.

7

When we turn to consider the divine precept, love your neighbour, we may perhaps draw a sigh of relief for this is familiar territory. We understand what it means and know how to practise it. To some extent, we are right; but, as we expose ourselves more fully to the truth of Jesus, we are less confident. I recall that, twenty years ago, I felt justified in making the claim that I did love others. It was made in a context, in relation to years of struggle against egotism and thus contained its own truth. Today, I find it impossible to make such a claim. I want to love others, I make it top priority and I do try, but what do I know of my deep motives? I think the area of charity towards others is one open to the greatest self-deception and subtlest form of self-seeking. However, this does not depress me. The God I know in Jesus is not one to reap where he never sowed, and this God knows our limitations, blindness and our deep fears of diminishment, together with the urge to assert ourselves, to give proof of our value and goodness. Our God knows we are creatures in the making, who are becoming and who grow step-by-step into truth and love. Our God knows that of ourselves we cannot emerge from this fearful self-centredness, and all the time is bending towards us in love, offering light, offering strength. It is on this I rely, not on my supposed purity of heart. I am sure that if we do our very best with the light we have, the Holy Spirit will look after it all for us.

And the likelihood of self-deception is not the only

problem. It is the sheer human impossibility – for we are not talking merely of our inborn neighbourliness and kindness, our natural sense of solidarity, which prompts us to all sorts of service for others. This is beautiful indeed and not without its divine spark, but the Christian concept of love transcends it, assumes it, but also infinitely expands it. Our precept is to love 'as I have loved you'. We are looking at love like God's love for us, unconditional and unto death, involving an opposite of self-possession, a being-for-others.

We are caught up into the divine sphere, committed to the divine plan to bring all things together in Christ, to share God's own life and happiness.

> Communion is the true nature of reality. The God we know is a 'holy communion', Trinity. The doctrine of the Trinity is not ultimately a teaching about 'God' but a teaching about God's life with us and our life with God . . . The life of God is not something which belongs to God alone. Trinitarian life is also our life . . . Followers of Christ are made sharers in the very life of God, partakers of divinity as they are transformed and perfected by the Spirit of God.[1]

There is:

> The one dynamic movement of God (the Father) outward, a personal self-sharing by which God is forever bending towards God's other.[2]

And there is:

> One ecstatic movement of God outward by which all things originate from God through Christ in the power of the Holy Spirit, and all things are brought into union with God and returned to God.[3]

The injunction 'Love one another' is saying 'Realise this truth.' Paul speaks of our 'realising' our common unity in Christ. What in principle we already are, we must, under the influence of the Holy Spirit, become. As Christians we must face up to our responsibility for the whole. We are not in relation to God as isolated individuals, caring for others because this is the way to serve God. We are in communion, one body in Christ. Though many – one. The way we respond to our vocation as members of Christ affects the whole body.

In this communion which is the 'holy communion' there are, literally, no distinctions. Here, such things as race, status, gender, age, have no importance. Each is a unique person called by name, eternally loved and destined for an eternal destiny. This is the truth that we must struggle to 'realise' in all the imperfections, distortions and frictional experiences of our daily life.

If we reflect long and carefully on the liturgy of the Mass: the eucharistic prayers, the prefaces, the prayers over the offering, and, indeed, the whole, rich, prayed theology of the missal, we shall gain an incomparable picture of our life in Christ. This is our supreme act of worship; it is the 'moment' of profoundest absorption into the holy Mystery. The Mass not merely expresses the Church's essence but we may truly say, makes us Church. The heart of this great sacrament is Jesus' surrender in love to his Father, for us and for our salvation. As we have already reflected, this 'happens' in the very heart of God and we are drawn into that heart. It is in the Mass that 'the grace of our Lord Jesus Christ, and the love of God [the Father] and the fellowship [communion] of the Holy Spirit' is with us.

Not that this holy Mystery is ever absent. Rather, in the midst of historical time there is always That which is beyond time; historical time flows within the timeless Ocean. But as creatures of time this eternal transaction of love is made concrete for us in the Mass. The Mass is the 'moment' for joining our 'Yes' to Jesus who, as Paul tells us, is himself the 'Yes', the great 'Amen' to the boundless plan of Love for creation. We do what we can: we bring our offerings which represent our very selves. We perform the rite Jesus gave us but it is to divine Love alone that we look for the transformation of the offerings of ourselves into the perfect offering of Jesus, the transformation of ourselves into the body of Christ.

> Let your Holy Spirit come upon these gifts to make them holy, so that they may become for us the body and blood of our Lord Jesus Christ.[4]

And:

> May all of us who share in the body and blood of Christ, be brought together in unity by the Holy Spirit.[5]

If we understood the Mass we would need no precept to bring us to participate in it. We would long to do so and daily if possible. The Mass of each day takes up into itself this one day and this one day then fulfils its eternal meaning of bringing us into more intimate 'holy communion', into the Trinity.

Catholicism is profoundly sacramental. In this way it, constantly, practically affirms that everything is given to us; our sanctification is a divine – not a human – work; we cannot make our own way to God but God has come to us in Jesus who himself has become our worship, our perfect offering, our union with the Father, our life, our holiness, our atonement.

A careful study of the liturgy of the sacraments will deepen our insight and we shall avoid the danger of seeing the sacraments as no more than sacred rites, duties we have to perform, in order to please God. Sadly, these wonderful, mystical gifts can fall into the category of meritorious works, a keeping of the law that gives us a claim on God. They are living, loving encounters, each one of them, with our Saviour, Jesus, who himself is one with God. Jesus is the important One. He is the giver, the doer, the offererer, the beloved of God. We come to the sacraments to be taken up in him. 'This is my body given for you. What I have done for you, you must do for others.' You too must be 'for others'. We come from the liturgy of the Mass and the other sacraments into the equally sacred liturgy of our daily lives. The sacramental character of the Church is a clear sign that there is no distinction between the sacred and the profane and that the whole of creation is holy and open to God.

> Each moment of our lives is like a grain of sand lying just alongside the ocean of mystery.[6]

As we have prayed at Mass, so we pray over our daily lives. We ask

> . . . you to make them holy by the power of your Spirit . . . [7]

and to

> . . . grant that we, who are nourished by the body and blood of Christ, may be filled with his Holy Spirit, and become one body, one spirit in Christ. May He make us an everlasting gift to you . . . [8]

For all of us, whatever our situation, love for our neighbour dissolves into tiny particularities or else it means nothing. If we pay attention we shall observe that our days present us with countless choices for selfishness or devotion to others; to self-interest, self-protectiveness and assertion, or promotion of the well-being of others. Such tiny instances! To my mind, it is attention to these tiny, unobtrusive things, hidden even from ourselves that have everything to do with love and are most likely to be free of self-deception. The letters of Paul (not to speak of John) have a great deal to say of practical Christian charity but we can note how the accent is on humility, putting others first, meekness, lowliness of heart, self-sacrifice – values not popular in ordinary society but the hallmark of Christians.

> Do nothing from selfishness or conceit, but in humility count others better than yourselves. Let each of you look not only to his own interests, but also to the interests of others.[9]

Paul does not hesitate to align our efforts to live our daily lives in sacrificial love with the kenosis of the Son of God. Paul is saying that in your daily living together, in the inevitable frictions, disagreements, temperamental differences, in the context of your own fears that others are, in all sorts of ways, a threat to yourselves, you must have the same mind as the Son of God who,

> though he was in the form of God, did not count equality with God a thing to be grasped, but emptied himself, taking the form of a servant.[10]

Paul carries the similitude on to the total emptying in love on the cross. How can we imagine we can do this of ourselves? We need the Mass, we need the sacraments, we need prayer.

Genuine love of our neighbour cannot be unthinking. We may not follow the natural, kind instincts of our hearts without examination, otherwise we shall be seeking ourselves, not our neighbour. We must try to discern with prayer, what is good for the other; the offer of a helping hand or the refusal? The 'kind' word or abrasive one? Encouragement or rebuke? It is hard to feel good when one has chosen to be 'hard'. When we have said 'No', withstood verbal abuse, given a rebuke. Nearly always, I experience a feeling of shame and self-reproach. It is difficult to refuse self-reflection afterwards, whereas the 'positive' acts – kind words, helping hands, meek responses – leave a glow behind. Every situation must be viewed in itself. There are no general rules; such as, we must always say the kind thing, always give the helping hand and so on. We would no doubt foster a nice self-image but we would not be loving our neighbour, at least not consistently.

The intense concern – often unrecognised – that good people have to keep their hands clean and their escutcheon untarnished is a serious obstacle to genuine love of neighbour and to our openness to God. It seems to me impossible to be really involved with others and at the same time feel that we are good. Jesus' immediate response to the appellation 'Good' was, 'Why do you call me good?'[11]

The gospels give us a picture of Jesus in constant interplay with others and these others are often hostile, crafty, sly, or trivial, blatantly self-seeking, blind; and then with his chosen disciples, obtuse, fickle, turning the most sacred moments into opportunities for self-glorification. Jesus was human. Jesus reacted to all these things before responding.

Response is a choice, reaction automatic. We have evidence of Jesus' anger, exasperation, and his sense of futility in what he was trying to do. Did he feel he was good, he who 'saw' his most holy Father? I cannot think so. He shared our lot, inevitably felt himself besmirched by our sinful attitude and ways and we cannot assume that he experienced all this as vicarious suffering. 'Only God is good.' Jesus saw this as no one else could. The closer we draw to Truth the more we realise this and, keeping our eyes on the 'only holy One' – our beloved Lord Jesus, he who in the midst of all his human struggles never wavered in obedience – we forget ourselves, cease to bother with our own self-image.

In all sorts of ways we use our neighbour for our own self-interest, even when we think we are most generous. Only exposure to Jesus will show us this. Subtly we manipulate others, demand that they be as we want them to be. Whilst our own 'I' dominates our lives, as naturally it does, we shall use others. We begin to discern, with pain perhaps, how sinful, how profoundly selfish we are and yearn for purification. If we truly desire it and beseech for it, most surely we shall receive it, but still we must try very, very hard in whatever ways we discern to forget our self-interest and give to others. I have come to attach great importance to the surrender of self-will in small matters when no principle is involved, but it is only a question of another's will confronting mine. Little power struggles go on all the time wherever people are together. Most of the time we hardly notice them, so much are they part of humanness. The instances may be trivial in the extreme and yet they are the arena for our exercise of power over others or our deliberate surrender of that power.

Living as I do in an enclosed community, I observe these little things. Someone is walking behind you, not wanting to dart out and pass, as that would be markedly discourteous but she certainly indicates that she would like you to get a move on, and instinctively you want to dig your heels in and continue at your chosen pace. Again, someone watching you peel vegetables suggests you hold the knife in a different way and you, aware that you have peeled vegetables since before she was born, would like to tell her so! Such trivialities! We all know

them or would do so if we paid attention. To repeat
Rahner, again:

> Each moment of our lives is like a grain of sand lying
> just alongside the ocean of mystery.[12]

And our response to that event is our response to the
Mystery that is love.

My own vocation is based on the truth of the communion of saints, of the intimate spiritual bonding of us all
and our mutual influence at the most spiritual, hidden
level. I understand that every time we surrender our own
will for power in no matter how trivial a situation, this
pervasive and destructive compulsion in humanity is
weakened. I believe that the more I surrender my whole
self to God, receive the purification which only the divine
Spirit can effect and become truly holy, the more the
whole body is sanctified.

We have a sacrament which exposes us to this purification. If we understand the meaning of God's forgiveness
we do not receive the sacrament of reconciliation to get
God to forgive us, but rather to celebrate the forgiveness
received. This demands an admission, within the body of
the Church, of our sinfulness. Here is our wonderful
opportunity for repairing the losses to the whole that our
selfishness has inflicted. We cannot repair them but Jesus
can and does. It is here that we can expose our sinful ten-
dencies, our hidden motives to the Spirit that searches the
heart, that knows our intimate selves as no one else can
and whose knowledge is all love. If only we realised how
blessed we are! If only we tried to look beyond the mere
appearances, beyond how we feel about things, whether
this or that appeals to us, to the inmost truth.

Faith is not make-believe; nor is it a matter of forming
mental images and calling them true. Faith is that which
pierces through appearances, through what seems, to

inmost reality and surrenders to it. We tend to stop short at the sense level: the imperfection and faultiness in the Church, in the liturgical celebration and the administration of the sacraments. We fail to see the wood for the trees. If we really understood God's gift of self in Jesus, the man, though we might be wounded by and grieve for the apparent sinful behaviour in the Church, we would not expect things to be different. How easily we would be beguiled by perfection in everything. Again, it would be our human selves, our own reflection, we were worshipping, not the divine Gift.

It is hardly likely that we shall enter fully into the sacramental life, receive the transforming action of God, unless we set aside some time exclusively for prayer. The whole of a truly Christian life is prayer. Prayer is simply laying ourselves open to receive God's gift, and that we can do every moment of the day and supremely in the Mass and in the other sacraments. It is doubtful though if this possibility can become an actuality unless we deliberately give a time when we put everything else aside, our own 'doings', and simply remain exposed to divine love. This is what we do at Mass in principle but, again, it would be difficult to realise this without a great deal of prayerful reflection and quite conscious effort to make explicit our faith in God's total availability, total will to give God's own Self.

At Mass, our attention can be absorbed by the ritual, by externals, and diverted from this inner disposition, unless we have attuned ourselves to becoming receptive. Every genuine Christian life calls for time for, what I shall call, 'exposed prayer'. The essence of prayer is what God does, what God gives. From the human side it is an attitude, a disposition, a willed desire to receive. It is a supreme act of faith for there is nothing whatever to justify such a 'waste of human time', save faith in the unseen, unperceived, in holy Mystery.

8

Our deepest reality as human beings is our relationship to God. It is what constitutes our identity as unique persons. What we experience of ourselves and our consciousness of who and what we are is largely illusory. God's intimate knowledge of us, the divine presence in the depth of our being, this is our truth and our 'Yes' to it is prayer. Prayer is God bending to us, offering us love, inviting us to intimate friendship.

This is true whether we know it or not. We cannot be out of the context for prayer because we cannot not be within this divine enfolding and self-offering of God. The holy Mystery is God-for-us, is God-for-me. God's call to us to receive love and be drawn into sacred intimacy is what defines our humanness. But this relationship can remain undeveloped. A baby in its mother's womb is in relationship with her but is unaware of it and does not respond to the mother's intense love and desire to give herself to her child. The relationship with God on the human side can remain as minimal as that of the baby. Love must be freely given, freely received and freely returned. This book is for those who, aware of this grounding relationship, want to make it the very meaning of their lives and open themselves to its fullest development.

If we really believe in the God Jesus shows to us then surely we must understand that our fundamental attitude or disposition must be to receive the love continually offered to us. God is not God-for-us on and off. God is always God, always loving us and working within us to enable us to respond to such love. This follows logically from what we have understood of the Father of Jesus. This communing will endure whenever we are in this fundamental disposition even though not fully conscious of it. I say this 'communing' and not 'presence' because God never leaves us even though we refuse to receive him. Communing involves mutuality and means we must want God, want to be open to the Holy Spirit's purifying and transforming action.

Our participation at Mass and our reception of the sacraments are moments full of possibility for intense communing. However, it is unlikely that we will maintain this fundamental choice of God, this orientation and the receptivity for God's gift of the divine Self unless we consciously advert to it, to the truth of our being, to our 'centre' – in other words, pray in the narrower sense of the word, actually give time to prayer, give the relationship our full attention in order for it to be the breath we breathe. If we have understood Jesus at all we must surely realise that prayer simply cannot be one activity alongside others. Prayer is our deepest reality, our relation to holy Mystery, our openness to the fullness of God. At the same time we must see how utterly simple it is. It is literally impossible to say anything at all about prayer itself, other than that it is the Holy Spirit of God giving God to us and giving us to God. This holy communion is, of its very nature, mystery; we are caught up in the holy Mystery that is Total Love.

The almost universal understanding of prayer is that it is something we do, it is our addressing God, our attempts to get an audience, our effort to reach God in some way. But we have seen, through considering what Jesus has to say, that this is only partly true. We are in the Father's house, we do not have to 'reach' God, God has come to be with us. All we have to do is to stay with God, remain there as the grateful recipients of the most tender love.

Our labour is to believe and never slacken in belief. Our faith must be grounded solely on Jesus and we must learn not to be in the least concerned that 'nothing seems to happen', that our senses are unaffected and our minds have no satisfying food and thus wander all over the place. There may, of course, be times when we are supported by consolations, when our feelings are in tune with the truth or our minds receive profound intuitions as to the reality of God's presence. These are blessed moments to encourage and strengthen us but we must not rely on them. Our feeling state may change, our perceptions vary, but the reality remains reality, and it is on this that we ground ourselves with every ounce of commitment. This blind clinging, this unswerving gaze into the 'nothing' that is holy Mystery, is saying in substance: 'You are God, Total Love. I am yours. Do with me, do in me whatever you please.' Julian of Norwich has a prayer that, I believe, is a perfect expression of a truly Christian understanding of God:

> God, of thy Goodness, give me thyself: for thou art
> enough to me, and I may nothing ask that is less that may
> be full worship to thee; and if I ask anything that is less,
> ever me wanteth, but only in thee have I all.[1]

Julian is saying in effect: 'Give thyself to me not because I am looking, not because I have worked hard to do your will and have given up everything for your sake, but simply and solely because you are who you are, the God who is pure self-giving Love.' What we are asking for is what does God desire with all the energy of his holy Self to give us and it is God who has made us understand that nothing less will ever satisfy our hearts.

What has been said so far could perhaps be interpreted as implying that prayer is only the real thing when we ourselves do nothing, remaining passive save for the 'reaching', the 'clinging' or 'watching' of faith, and that methods of any kind are to be eschewed. In no way is this so. My purpose has been to insist on the essence of prayer and on how important it is that we constantly bear it in mind. We must convince ourselves that prayer is God's work first and last, and the logical conclusion is that our part must be to receive.

Once this truth is firmly established then everything falls into place. Each one of us has to discover how best to maintain this fundamental attitude of faith and surrender to the silent, hidden Mystery of love always intent on us. The humble means we employ will vary according to our temperament or perhaps our stage of growth. No one can decide for another and at best we can only suggest or share our own experience. We must watch, though, that we are not trying to control our prayer. That is the danger with all our methods. Instead of using them 'lightly', not to impress God in any way but to enable our wayward, easily disorientated self to be gathered up, focused, we use them as barricades behind which we can hide, defending ourselves from God. In practice, this means protecting ourselves from feeling inadequate, helpless, 'at sea', a mere 'brute beast', in God's presence. I, for instance, would have little difficulty in passing a very rewarding hour with a train of thought such as I would have were I planning to address a conference or write a chapter of this book. My thoughts would be of God and might be profound, but I would know quite well that I would be shirking prayer. Good as it is (and, at the proper time, God's will and therefore prayer) to engage in it as a substitute for exposed prayer is, I know, infidelity. There was a time, when, sick and tired of my butterfly mind, I decided to try a simple method for stilling it. Again, I realised that this too was an escape. In a subtle way my attention was on myself, on my effort to keep my mind quiet – basically, so that I would feel better! Now, I am quite certain that, if we intend to give the allotted time to being with God and do not deliberately withdraw that intention then, no matter how it seems to us, we can be sure that God is lovingly working within us.

Our methods, the scaffolding we use to support ourselves, must never be confused with prayer itself or given much importance. That this is a common error hardly needs saying. It lies behind all our confusions and anxieties regarding prayer, our yearning for reassurance, for someone to teach us how to get it right. It lies behind the complaints: 'I cannot pray', 'My prayer is hopeless.' It is the source of all discouragement. Our attention is on ourselves. We are centre-stage and our entertainment of God is what matters and what a mess we are making of it! How, oh, how, can we improve our performance?

Inevitably, we feel badly about ourselves: miserable, unspiritual. It is quite impossible that the holy God would be interested in such as us. We must do something about improving ourselves before we can risk exposing ourselves to God. God must not see our naked reality! The irony of it! For us, the Holy Spirit is not around. We are labouring outside the family home. If we bear in mind the essence of prayer and confront our difficulties and anxieties, we shall see that these have nothing to do with prayer, but only with our false expectations and lack of faith. What divine Love wants us to do is to take our eyes off ourselves and fix them on Jesus, and spread out our anxieties beneath his gaze.

It is just these disappointments – with ourselves – that offer us the chance of real growth. The 'dark nights' are, at bottom, nothing but our own preoccupation with ourselves, the collapse of our expectations, the unmasking of our 'God' and the disappearance of this image of our own fashioning. They are meant to be the beginning of genuine faith, faith not in ourselves, our own notions of God, but in the holy Mystery Jesus reveals. They are invitation, the Holy Spirit's drawing us into Truth. We have to choose: go on hunting desperately for certainties, for comforting inner assurances – go on until we hit upon that which affords them, or surrender blindly to the dark, putting all our trust in the God of Jesus.

This is where many, many say 'No', at least to some extent. It is the summoning to that self-denial Jesus speaks of, a letting go of our own life in order to have 'eternal' life, God's own life. If we want God to be our All then our ego has to die. If we are to live by divine energy, then we must surrender – allow divine Love to take away (or, rather, transform) our own inner springs. It means we must stop clinging to our own perceptions, demanding to stay within our own capabilities, insisting on a deity we can manage. We have to accept to have nothing whatsoever of our own. Since our profoundest reality, our for-Godness, is concealed from normal perception and is a pure gift of God that we cannot manipulate or 'possess', so the mysterious work of our transformation and the substitution of the divine for the merely human, take place in deepest secrecy. Blind trust in Love can be the only answer.

A simple consequence of this is that we must be content not to enjoy our spiritual life. Paul has a striking image. In a magnificent passage he writes of the God who said, 'Let light shine out of darkness', who has shone in our hearts to give the

> light of the knowledge of the glory of God in the face of Christ.[2]

This, the supreme communication of God to us. But, he continues,

> . . . we have this treasure in earthen vessels to show that the transcendent power belongs to God and not to us.[3]

101

So, we are clay pots! We do not like being clay pots! We would like to be nice vessels, shapely, of precious metal, finely wrought. No, says Paul, just a clay pot. We would like to think there was a certain fitness about our being selected to hold the treasure, that our work on ourselves had made us, if not worthy, at least not unworthy to receive it. Clay pot, says Paul. It is the treasure that is important. Give that all your attention, never mind the pot.

True spirituality is unselfconscious. I am very far from saying we are to be caught up in rapture. No one could lay less claim to that than I who have never experienced such a thing in all my life. Rather, it means that, in practice, we pray, not to see ourselves praying or enjoy ourselves praying. True prayer takes place in our inaccessible depths. Anything we experience can only be a sort of backwash of it whether joy-giving or painful. It is unimportant. My experience is of a bit of washed-up flotsam and I could become utterly exasperated, heartily sick of myself, because my mind jumps about all over the place. I never have the satisfaction of feeling that I have prayed, nor even the certainty that I have been faithful. Indeed, I have no certainties at all about myself except that I am loved by God and that God's love can be relied upon to purify, transform me and finally complete the work. I do not ask for any proof of this but am content to believe it. I used to be as upset as anyone and terribly anxious until I learned to live by Jesus' truth. Now it does not worry me. I am quite content. I understand clearly that whenever I feel spiritual aches and pains, a general fed-up-ness with Godly matters, it is myself I am sick of. It is quite impossible to become bored with God, to be disgusted with God. It is simply that, as yet, I cannot catch the beauty, the glory, the bliss of the holy Mystery, but I know It Is, and that is enough.

When I realise that, my own experience of my poor

self matters little, it is telling me nothing of significance. It is impossible to be outside the embrace of the holy Mystery and that which I perceive as 'nothing' is, in fact, All. The sense of God's absence, of God not being there, which can be so afflictive for us who try to live for God, is only telling us that, mercifully, the God that is no God but only our own fabrication, satisfies us no longer. The God that is the God of our heart simply cannot be absent. Our sense of loss becomes an invitation to find, or rather lose, ourselves in the real God. These aches and pains, all these difficulties that leave us feeling spiritually impoverished must be quietly endured. To run away from them into self-satisfying forms of prayer (which are only fantasies) or into abandoning prayer altogether in order to do 'something more useful' for God (that leaves us our decent self-image as a spiritual person) is to betray the holy Mystery that is drawing us so powerfully.

If we remind ourselves over and over again of what prayer is in essence and try to act accordingly, we shall transcend all these superficial yet trying states of feeling. Truly, I am convinced that everything we can experience by way of spiritual, psychic, emotional (call it what you will) difficulty, must be seen simply as self-preoccupation and, without any dallying with it, be let drop as we surrender to Mystery. Yet each of us tends to feel that our particular difficulty is the exception and demands attention and ought to be a cause of concern. If that is true, the answer is simple – correct what is wrong! If we find that, in fact, we cannot correct it, let it drop.

Immersed in the Mystery of love, even though there be not the slightest awareness of it, or rather because there is no awareness, nothing therefore that is our own, no finite image, we are blessedly safe.

In his novel, *The Eye of the Storm*, Patrick White has one of his characters experience this remarkable phenomenon:

> For several hours we were thrown and battered, till
> suddenly calm fell – the calmest calm I have ever
> experienced at sea. God had willed us to enter the
> eye – the still centre of the storm – where we lay at rest,
> surrounded by hundreds of seabirds also resting on the
> waters.[4]

In my often distressing mental and emotional turmoils,
like one of the seabirds, I know where to go: I fly into the
Eye and rest calmly on the waters.

This does not mean that I am no longer aware of the
storm – sometimes yes, often no. It is only that the part
of me that can choose has taken off in a flight of faith to
that unshakeable, inaccessible depth where God is God-
for-me. I believe we can all do that: take a flight of faith
away from any preoccupation with the 'storm', whatever
its nature, into the absolute calm of God.

Arthur Ransome, too, has a fine image for us in his
children's novel *Mr Duck*. The youthful sailors are caught
in a violent storm off the Bay of Biscay, and the seasoned
old sailor, Mr Duck, takes charge. He heaves the small
boat to, everything is battened down, the engine is
switched off and the boat is abandoned to the storm. 'She
will lie as snug as a gull,' Mr Duck assures the children as
he sends them down below to sleep. And sure enough the
small boat does:

> She lay quiet, meeting the waves as they came, but no
> longer driven on her way.[5]

A deep lesson for us!

> *Rocked in the cradle of the deep*
> *I lay me down in peace to sleep.*
> *Secure I rest upon the waves . . .* [6]

And, of course, we have the unforgettable picture of Jesus asleep in the boat, in a storm of such violence that the experienced fishermen were panic stricken. This is how Jesus, in his inmost heart, lived in trust throughout the tempest that was his mortal life.

How removed this is from all fascination with our 'spiritual life'! Often, when people speak or write on prayer there is the impression that it is an interesting dimension of life. Real life goes on as usual, but alongside it is this fascinating business of prayer and particularly contemplative prayer. How different the real thing, when prayer is understood as the whole of life, everything assumed into it: time, thought, attention, direction, every faculty employed towards the Beloved, the God of our heart. A true spiritual life, a life that is prayer, is all about love, love received and love given; lack of concern for self, total concern for the other. It moves inexorably along the path of dispossession, selflessness, the surrender of autonomy to the Beloved.

Pride is the enemy of love and is the root of all sin. At bottom it is a denial of creaturehood. It is that impulse, so powerful, so much part of ourselves that mostly we do not notice it except in its grosser manifestations – 'I must be allowed to be myself.' Our vital forces are constantly on the alert to be who we think we are, to get what we think we need and have a right to. We conjure up an image of what a human being is and set about moulding ourselves into that idea. This self-planning is carried right into our spiritual life. In all this we are really asserting that we do not need God. We need God to give the finishing touches, and our self-perfecting must take place within the bright aura of God. We fail to see that we are actually designing God as well as ourselves. Of course, in our heads, we all know differently, but what I have described is no caricature.

The cure lies with God alone. We could not perceive

105

how to cure ourselves. Even when we begin to suspect the self-seeking motives dominating our spiritual endeavour, and that is a gift of grace, our own efforts can achieve nothing. They would only reinforce the power of ego. God must take us in hand and is all readiness to do so. Our faithful daily exposure to God such as I have tried to suggest gives God the best chance. Divine Love will use everything in our lives as a purifying agent but we must be on the alert and not shirk the self-revelation it brings, but receive it in peace.

This true dying to self we simply cannot preconceive without mystical enlightenment; it is a participation in the dying and rising of Jesus. We cannot initiate it, still less achieve it. What we can do on the practical level is learn to love others unselfishly, be faithful in prayer, desire and humbly wait. Salvation will come.

Walter Brueggeman quotes from Ezekiel:

> It is not for your sake, O house of Israel, that I am about
> to act, but for the sake of my holy name . . . I will
> vindicate the holiness of my great name . . . and the
> nations will know that I am the Lord, says the Lord God,
> when through you I vindicate my holiness before their
> eyes.[7]

And:

> It is not for your sake that I will act, says the Lord God;
> let that be known to you.[8]

Brueggeman comments penetratingly on these two texts: 'Only holiness gives hope.'[9] He, shows, too, that precisely in these uncompromisingly harsh statements, Israel's absolute security lies. Ezekiel has written with flaming pen and outraged heart of the infidelity, the scorn for Yahweh and his love, the sheer wickedness of the chosen people. Yet Yahweh intends to save them. Nothing whatsoever they have done has merited such an act – how could they doubt that! Israel no longer has any call upon God; her harlotry, her constant betrayals have wiped out the covenant. Yet Yahweh intends to save, to vindicate his own holiness.

> The holiness of God serves only God. It has no other purpose, no other partner to take into account. It enters no other service. It cannot be harnessed or presumed upon. For Ezekiel, God is not one who gives God's self away . . . But how odd. This God is inalienably related to Israel and has no life apart from this people. This God will not be enhanced, except by acts towards Israel . . . [10]

Ezekiel's insight is profound. The very nature of God, for God to be as God is, demands that Israel must be saved, Israel must be raised from the dead, 'not for your sake, but for mine'.[11] And:

> The load is lifted. We begin again, the bones rattle, the air stirs . . . [12]

The utterly free and sovereign One, whom no one can manipulate, on whom no one makes a claim, cannot *not* be God of Israel and save. Unshakeable security lies only in God's own way of being God.

Bring this forward into the light that Jesus sheds and how infinitely richer it is. The Truth, the only meaning and purpose for all that is, is to manifest, to glorify, God's love. When we hear such 'hard nosed' statements as 'God seeks God's glory', 'God acts only for God's glory', this is what is being said. We learn through Jesus that God is Total Love and nothing less. For God to glorify the divine Reality means God must love and love and love unto complete self-emptying. As we have seen already, the human, this-worldly expression of God's self-expending love is Jesus dying on the cross. Herein lies our absolute security. This security is unshakeable, founded on the bedrock of the eternal God. There is nothing precarious, nothing changeable, nothing that depends on something else. It is itself its own unshakeable ground. If we understand our Christian vocation we shall see that it is finely expressed in Ephesians:

> We are destined to live to the praise of his glorious grace.'[13]

God is glorified precisely when we allow God to be God to us, Total Love.

Lashed by Ezekiel's unsparing tongue, the people of Israel could only admit that there was nothing in themselves to incite God to save them. Jesus himself, and the New Testament writers likewise, strip us of all our pretentious claims. We are given bedrock security, but not of ourselves, an unbreakable fidelity. Yet we find it almost impossible to leave off our search for something to show for ourselves, something within ourselves that we can rely on. We let go in one area only to discover that we are waving our little claim in another.

I think many earnest people, if they were to reflect upon it, would admit that they perceive God as always asking, with love, with tenderness, 'What are you giving me? What are you doing for me?' And this creates anxiety and the response: 'What can I do for God? What more can I give? How can I prove my generosity?' I think it was this anxiety that prompted the self-inflicted penances of the past. They afforded a sense of generosity, of doing something for God. But, of course, the only person we are trying to convince is ourself. If God is in any way conceived as asking that question then the proper response is: 'Nothing, dear Lord, only the desire to receive.'

My own vocation to Carmel has shown me this. I used to feel that questioning and consequent anxiety and yet, in Carmel, I had nothing to offer. A Carmelite has no external apostolate; nothing heroic to give to God. And I began to perceive that my vocation was simply to be there to receive, and that I must, for love, renounce all desire to 'give God something'. I understand too that this renunciation belongs to the Christian vocation as such. No matter what our external works for God, our inmost heart must know that these must be 'hidden' from self, and that the heart's emptiness, its receptivity, is what matters and ensures the holiness of the works.

How unhappy we feel, how fearful, when we cannot see ourselves as good, when our supposed virtue crumbles, when our profound weakness is laid bare! We are quite devastated. What more important aim have we than to struggle to ground ourselves on our one sole security? There is no other way of glorifying God. Jesus has made that so clear. All God wants of us is complete trust. Most good people establish a *via media*. They trust God in all sorts of ways but never wholly, never to the extent that they throw themselves overboard, and really this reveals that their 'God' is not the holy Mystery, but a God honed down to their own capabilities.

It would be rare, I think, to find someone who, from the very start, has sought only God, whose religious striving has been purely for the praise of God's glory. Only gradually are we led to perceive that we are using God for our own glorification.

This enlightenment is the work of the Holy Spirit and comes in all sorts of ways and can hardly be painless, since it strikes at the very roots of self-love, self-preservation and autonomy. Not infrequently, it must cut right across nature's course. Will we accept the light? Will we allow ourselves to be cleansed of our idols (we have only one idol really – ourself), and to be drawn into the holy land

109

where all is pure God? We saw that Jesus, in order to become who he really was in all fullness, seemed mysteriously to be deprived of what made him human. In union with the Beloved, something similar must happen to us.

Paul speaks of

> . . . we all, with unveiled face, beholding the glory of the Lord, are being changed into his likeness from one degree of glory to another.[14]

What is the glory of the Lord but self-emptying Love? It is John who emphatically insists that the supreme moment of divine Glory was when Jesus died on the cross. This is the glory we must 'catch'. We too must go out of ourselves completely in love. As Paul insists, this can be accomplished only by the Spirit. This is what is meant by 'sharing the divine nature'.

Divine Love comes to us; comes, undefended, as Its pure self into our sinful world. 'Come to me!' Beauty beyond what mind and heart can conceive appears in this world as a human love that is all-offer, unarmed vulnerability itself. Inevitably, so total, so excessive is the self-emptying, that he stands before us 'without beauty, without majesty'. We look on him and . . . ?

That is the question of all questions. Do we recognise here the divine? Do we see limitless love? Or do we look for it elsewhere in what our minds, our senses, perceive as beautiful and godly? Before this vision our spiritual pretensions must fall away, all desire to have a holiness we can ourselves enjoy. We discern that to love defenceless Love demands the willingness to be like Love. Beauty and majesty are expected of holiness and it is bitter and self-emptying to accept that they will be markedly absent; and, thus, do many go away and walk no more with him.

In Jesus there has come to us 'news of a great joy',[15]

such 'eternal comfort, and good hope through grace'[16]. But this joy can only be received by the 'little ones', those who are willing to lay aside their own wisdom and under-standing to be lit solely by Jesus whom God has made our wisdom. This wisdom is at odds with the wisdom of this world; to that it seems sheer folly. This divine folly, which is God's wisdom, leads us gently along the path that the Son of God, holy Wisdom, took – the path of selfless love. Lit by this secret wisdom that comes from the very heart of God, we know the very mind of God, the same mind that was in Christ Jesus.

Lit by this holy Wisdom, we disclaim anything as of ourselves. Jesus alone is our holiness. We look for none within ourselves – ever – and this is our security. It is God who has done all: given us Jesus, given us everything in him. What seems like death is life. Only those who really allow God to make Christ Jesus their wisdom and their holiness can know unshakeable security. Relying on nothing whatsoever within themselves or anything cre-ated, they can never be let down. They are free.

> Freedom takes place only in the unconditional, loving acceptance of God as God is . . . when God by grace grants to the free, finite subjects to abandon themselves in love to incomprehensibility of God without the will to return once again to the false autonomy of self.[17]

To speak in my simpler language and in the imagery I love: our inmost heart rests always in the eye of the storm. We are spared nothing of life's burdens; shed tears as others do. We too can feel stretched to our limits and beyond, but all the while, that which is deepest in us is with God. Divine Love continually upholds the fragile creature that has risked all for its sake. This is, I believe, the perfection of faith: a divine empowering, a divine sus-taining and a divine holding. Consciousness may know only what natural knowledge knows, but holy Mystery is Home. There we stay, suffering its 'darkness', wanting no escape, waiting for the moment

> . . . when its overpowering acuteness is no longer able to be suppressed, but must be sustained and endured as it is in itself.[18]

And this will be total bliss.

Notes

Preface

1. Job 38:1.
2. Ps 139:1.
3. *Orientale Lumen*. Cf. Jn 8:55.
4. K. Rahner, 'The Concept of Mystery in Catholic Theology', *Theological Investigations*, Vol IV.
5. Catherine Mowry LaCugna, *God for Us*.
6. Ibid.
7. 1 Jn 4:8.

Chapter 1

1. Rahner, 'The Concept of Mystery in Catholic Theology'.
2. E. Schillebeeckx, *Jesus*.
3. LaCugna, *God for Us*.
4. Eccles 1:14–17.
5. Ibid., 8:16–17.
6. Rahner, 'The Concept of Mystery in Catholic Theology'.
7. Omitted from the author's published edition, *Before the Living God*.
8. Rahner, 'The Concept of Mystery in Catholic Theology'.
9. Ibid.
10. J. A. T. Robinson, *The Human Face of God*.
11. Cf. 1 Jn:1.
12. Eph 1:4.
13. Rom 8:30.

14. Cf. Is 61:10. Used in the liturgy of both feasts.
15. W. Kaspar, *Jesus the Christ.*

Chapter 2

1. Gen 6:5–7.
2. Ps 37:25–34.
3. Ibid., 44:17–18.
4. Job 29:2–5.
5. Ibid., 42:15.
6. Ibid.
7. Ibid., 9:11.
8. Ibid., 14:15.
9. Ps 73:2.
10. Ibid., 73:23–26.
11. Is 52:15.
12. Ibid., 53:5–6.
13. 1 Pet 2:22.
14. Is 38:18–19.
15. Ps 16:9–11.
16. Ibid., 139:8.
17. J. Zizioulas, *Being as Communion.*
18. Ibid.
19. Ibid.
20. Ps 63:1–3.
21. I have paraphrased this passage. Cf. Job 38:41.
22. Cf. 1 Tim 1:10.

Chapter 3

1. Jn 6:44.
2. Julian of Norwich, *Revelations of Divine Love.*
3. Eph 1:9–10.
4. Zizioulas, *Being as Communion.*

114

5. Gal 1:16.
6. Wis 7:7–9.
7. Ibid., 7:26.
8. Mt 11:27.
9. LaCugna, *God for Us.*
10. Deut 6:4–7.
11. Lk 12:34.
12. St John of the Cross.
13. Mk 4:24.
14. I have paraphrased this passage. Cf. Jn 16:13.

Chapter 4

1. Fr Faber. From his hymn, *O Come and mourn with me awhile.*
2. Heb 4:11–13.
3. Jn 15:9.
4. 1 Jn 2:27.
5. Sister Wendy Beckett.
6. Ps 45:2.
7. Lk 4:22.
8. Jn 7:46.
9. I have paraphrased this passage. Cf. Wis 7:22–24.
10. Wis 7:25.
11. Mk 4:30.
12. Jn 6:66.
13. Ibid., 7:1.
14. Cf. Heb 5:7.
15. Ibid., 2:11.
16. Ibid., 2:13.

Chapter 5

1. Mt 13:3.

2. Cf. Mt 22.
3. Mt 23:10.
4. Jn 14:8.
5. Ibid., 6:63.
6. Ibid., 14:26.
7. 2 Cor 5:19.
8. Mt 9:2–8. For the phrase 'my son', Jesus may have said 'my child'; or maybe we would best translate it today as 'my dear'.
9. Mt 4:23. See also 9:35.
10. Ibid., 15:30.
11. Lk 2:10.
12. Mt 11:28–30.
13. Song 2:14.
14. Rom 3:22–23.
15. K. E. Bailey, *Poet and Peasant Through Peasant Eyes*.

Chapter 6

1. Mt 20:1.
2. Sister Wendy Beckett. Unpublished work.
3. Cf. Lk 13:29.
4. Mt 5:17–43.
5. Ibid., 25:14–28.
6. Lk 16:1–8.
7. Cf. Bailey, *Poet and Peasant Through Peasant Eyes*.
8. Rahner, 'The Concept of Mystery in Catholic Theology'.
9. Col 2:2–3.
10. 2 Cor 5:19.
11. LaCugna, *God for Us*.
12. W. Brueggemann, *Prophetic Imagination*. Brueggemann is here quoting Jer 9:1.
13. Phil 2:7.
14. Heb 2:9–10.
15. Ibid., 5:8–9.

16. H. Guest, 'Triumphal Entry', *Words from Jerusalem.*

Chapter 7

1. LaCugna, *God for Us.*
2. Ibid.
3. Ibid.
4. Eucharist prayer 2.
5. Ibid.
6. K. Rahner, *Liturgy of the World.*
7. Eucharist prayer 3.
8. Ibid.
9. Phil 2:3–4.
10. Ibid., 2:6–7.
11. Cf. Mk 10:18.
12. Rahner, *Liturgy of the World.*

Chapter 8

1. Julian of Norwich, *Revelations of Divine Love.*
2. 2 Cor 4:6.
3. Ibid., 4:7.
4. P. White, *The Eye of the Storm.*
5. A. Ransome, *Mr Duck.*
6. Anon. These lines are from memory; taken from an old Victorian (?) song book that was in my house when I was a child.
7. Brueggemann, *Prophetic Imagination.* Brueggemann is here quoting Ezek 36:22–23.
8. Ezek 36:32.
9. Brueggemann, *Prophetic Imagination.*
10. Ibid.
11. Cf. Ezek 36:22.
12. Brueggemann, *Prophetic Imagination.*

13. Eph 1:6.
14. 2 Cor 3:18.
15. Lk 2:10.
16. 2 Thess 2:16.
17. Rahner, 'The Concept of Mystery in Catholic Theology'.
18. Ibid.